HAPPIER FAMILIES

HAPPIER FAMILIES

Raising Responsible, Self-managed Children

Michael B. Medland, Ph.D.

BARCROFT Publishing

San Francisco

Publisher's Cataloging-in-Publication Data

Medland, Michael B.
  Happier families: raising responsible, self-managed
  children / by Michael B. Medland

      p.   cm.

  Includes index
  ISBN 0-9633009-6-2
  1. Parent and child.   2. Child rearing.
  3. Self-control in children.   4. Domestic education.
  I. Title.   II. Raising responsible, self-managed children.
  HQ769.M395   1992   649'.1 — dc20   92-081926

Library of Congress Catalog Card Number: 92-081926
ISBN: 0-9633009-6-2

First published in 1992

Barcroft Publishing, San Francisco, CA 94121
Printed in the United States of America

10 9 8 7 6 5 4 3 2 1

DEDICATION

To children and parents

To the work and memory of BFS

ACKNOWLEDGEMENTS

Thanks go to Mark Hubbard for his editorial effort. Trying to make my writing readable is a Herculean task. Thanks also go to Susan Hubbard for her support.

CONTENTS

CHAPTER 1

SELF-MANAGEMENT

Besides clear values and consistent love, self-management is the most important advantage you can give your children to help insure their future success and happiness. They already have access to the other skills they need to achieve a better life. Resources abound in the form of private and public schools, bookstores and libraries, apprenticeship programs, colleges and universities. They can be trained to become anything from architects to zoologists. What's currently missing is instruction on how to manage themselves along the way, how to achieve not only academic excellence but a healthier, more responsible and secure family life.

Self-management supports you in completing tasks and solving problems. In this opening chapter, I briefly introduce both the language and procedures of self-management. The language enables you to communicate—the procedures enable you to act.

SELF-MANAGEMENT AS A SET OF STRATEGIES

There are seven skills that manage an activity. I call these *strategies* because they have specific steps that facilitate the performance of a task, whether it's washing dishes, building a chair, balancing a checkbook, or going to the moon. The seven self-management strategies are planning, learning, organizing, supervising, intervening, helping, and sharing.

Planning

The planning strategy gives you a way to get the job done. It does so by identifying activities and associated problems, building and selecting solutions, and evaluating the outcomes. The solution may work completely or require revision. If the latter is true, planning begins again, but with the new knowledge gained from having implemented and evaluated the plan. Planning can be done individually or by a group. When done in a group, it is often called participative management, which is especially well suited for families.

Learning

There are times when everyone needs to learn. We may not know how to perform the activity task—the cleaning, repairing, painting, building—or one of the self-management strategies. We must change ourselves so that we can see and affect the world differently than in the past. The learning strategy guides learners in changing so they can reenter planning or performing an activity with an increased chance of success.

The learner begins by identifying the learning problem. Once identified, he or she gathers and organizes the learning sources that could help. Next, the learner "unpacks" these sources to find the relevant knowledge that each contains. To begin, the child asks the parent a question or an adult goes to the index of a book. Once the knowledge is found and extracted, the learner must "pack" it. The packing directly links what was learned with the learning problem. At more advanced stages, each step of learning requires a number of supporting skills, like using card catalogs or bibliographies to locate sources, and outlining and summarizing to pack the knowledge found.

Organizing

When self-managers think they can perform the activity, they begin to organize the resources required. They must first identify what needs to be organized. This includes time, people, materials and tools. Once identified, these resources must be located in the surrounding environment. When a child hunts for crayons and paper to begin a drawing or asks others where they are, she is locating. An adult may use the phone book or other references. The next step is to transfer the resources to the location of the activity at the appropriate time. Once the resources are at the activity location, they are arranged for easy use and returned to their pre-activity location when finished.

Supervising

Supervisors initiate, maintain, and end the actual activity performance. They focus on guiding the actions, or behaviors, of those involved. Supervisors first identify the need to supervise. They may have to help set task goals, insure that everyone knows the plan, direct activity flow, look for success, or point out the consequences of performance. Successful managers not only supervise their own activities expertly, but can adjust their supervision to a variety of individuals.

Intervening

Families experience many kinds of conflicts. Conflicts are counterproductive behaviors that stop activities from moving ahead. To resolve conflicts in a fair and lasting way, families need an intervening strategy. The strategy involves five steps. Potential interveners must identify when a conflict exists and move to stop it. To insure that it does not recur, better or more appropriate ways to behave are found, preferably by the disputants. Practicing these better ways increases the chance of appropriate behavior in the future. If the conflict has persisted, put others in danger, or damaged property, a settlement may be needed. The last step is to document the conflict, the better way, and the settlement, if necessary.

The specific details will depend on your intervention skills and those of your family. In the beginning, for example, the parent will function as an arbitrator, making most of the decisions. As the disputants gain some skills, the intervener will serve as a mediator, getting those involved to participate as much as possible. When the disputants are skilled, they can stop and negotiate the elimination of conflicts themselves. Teaching children to resolve their own conflicts requires gradually leading them from arbitration to mediation, and finally to negotiation.

Helping

With helping, activities continue without interruption. Children, for example, can help a parent set the table, carry in the groceries, or assist in caring for younger siblings. To initiate helping, the first step is to recognize the need. Either the helper or the helpee (the one who needs help) can make this determination and offer to (or ask for) help. If accepted, helping can proceed and ends in thanks. Both helper and helpee initiated forms of helping are important.

Sharing

Within and across activities, resources are often in short supply. Whatever the reason for their scarcity, a little sharing often allows everyone to continue. When children can't share, the results are often complaints, whining, temper tantrums, or conflicts. All of these stop an activity.

Sharing is much like helping. The sharer or sharee must first see the need to share, and then request or offer to share. With acceptance, sharing ensues and ends with returning that which is shared. It is the diligent care of shared property and its prompt return that is important in avoiding later conflicts.

The figure on the facing page displays the strategies and identifies their steps. In Chapters 6 through 12, I divide each strategy step into several smaller steps called *elements*, and show you how to teach them to your children. Chapter 3 provides the procedures to analyze your family activities. It is within these activities that the learning and teaching of self-management take place. Chapter 10 outlines family activity planning.

SELF-MANAGEMENT AS A SYSTEM

The seven self-management strategies work together. They form a system to manage activity performance. It is their systemic nature that gives the strategies their power across a wide range of activities.

SELF-MANAGEMENT STRATEGIES
———————— The Strategies and Their Component Steps ————————

PLANNING	LEARNING	ORGANIZING	SUPERVISING
▼	▼	▼	▼
Identify the Problem	Identify the Problem	Identify the Resources	Identify the Need
Design Solutions	Organize Sources	Locate the Resources	Tell About the Plan
Select a Solution	Unpack Knowledge	Transfer the Resources	Set Activity Goals
Evaluate the Solution	Pack Knowledge	Arrange the Resources	Direct Activity Flow
			Look for Success
			Describe Consequences

INTERVENING
▼
Identify the Need
Stop the Conflict
Find a Better Way
Settle the Conflict
Document the Conflict

HELPING
▼
Identify the Need
Offer or Ask for Help
Accept or Reject
Help as Needed

SHARING
▼
Identify the Need
Offer or Ask for Sharing
Accept or Reject
Share as Needed

The figure on the next page shows how the strategies work together. Activities move from planning to organizing to supervising. If you can't complete the plan or follow it with success, you turn to the learning strategy. Once you think your plan can be followed, you turn to organizing and supervising. You use intervening, helping, and sharing only when needed. After a task has been completed, you return to planning if further change is required.

When the activity environment remains stable, the performance of a task goes unchanged and the systematic nature of self-management goes unnoticed. Washing dishes provides an example. If you go camping, the activity environment changes and so does the routine performance of the dishwashing. You must manage yourself differently than you did at home. You stop, plan, and organize for this new environment so you can wash the dishes.

Once an activity becomes routine, the self-management behaviors become invisible. You may think about the task behaviors of scrubbing, rinsing, wiping, and putting away. Yet, the first time you entered your kitchen, you planned how the dishes would be done. You organized the elements needed for the task—the soap, pans, scrubbers, and dish towels.

SELF-MANAGEMENT SYSTEM
──── A Model of How the Strategies Work Together ────

TASK/PROBLEM ACTIVITY
── Within Home, School, Leisure, or Work Life ──

LEARN ← no

PLAN → Can The Plan Be Followed? yes → ORGANIZE → SUPERVISE

INTERVENE, HELP, SHARE ←
──── Use When Needed ────

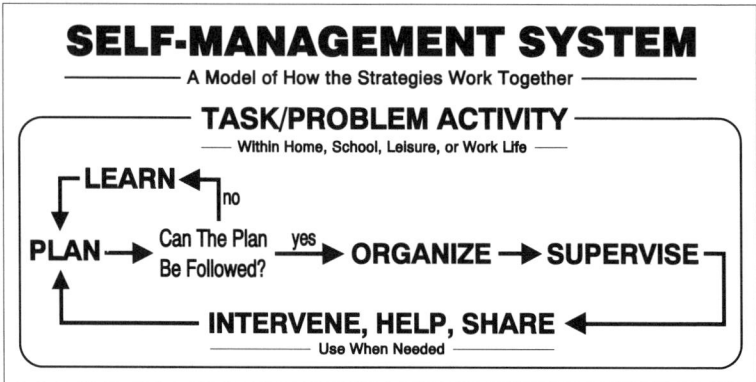

At holidays or big meals, the environmental conditions change again. You have more dishes to do. You ask for help and distribute the task of doing the dishes with others. You supervise those involved by asking them how they want to contribute, identifying where to put the dishes, and coordinating their movements from beginning to end. You may even have to stop a conflict if a son or daughter does not want to participate. These self-management behaviors may seem minor, but only because you have done them many times in the past and have seen them done holiday after holiday by your parents and relatives, who have supplied you with a "plan."

The world requires much more of us than managing tasks like washing dishes, and our children will enter an even more complex world. Teaching yourself and your children the seven self-management strategies as a system across a wide range of activities will give your family a great advantage.

CHAPTER 2

PRINCIPLES OF FAMILY

I began exploring self-management when I was an elementary school teacher. Over time, I realized that simply learning to manage oneself individually or in a group was not enough. Both the doctor and the drug dealer can be well managed, but the consequences of their behaviors are certainly different for themselves and for society. I wanted my students not only to achieve personal success, but also to contribute to the well-being of their families and the larger community. As a parent, you probably share this same goal. To help you obtain it, I have formulated a few principles of conduct. I offer them to support and assist you in raising responsible, self-managed children.

WHAT PRINCIPLES?

What principles will you select to guide the conduct of your family? Where will you begin? You could review historical documents, like the Declaration of Independence, the Bill of Rights, the Constitution of the United States, and the Charter of the United Nations. You might turn to religious books and teachings. There are even fictional influences, like Isaac Asimov's principles of robotics and Gene Roddenberry's directives for the Starship Enterprise. Some of these sources may be more useful than others, but all have something important to say about conduct. The problem is that most were not written from the perspective of the daily life of the family. Often, they fail to specify both rights and responsibilities.

Put together the sources that interest you, along with the definitions of valued ideas like freedom, equality and harmony. Next, study and summarize them, and eventually reduce the lot to a set of principles. That is what I have done. Use the following Principles of Family as offered, or as a framework for developing your own.

THE PRINCIPLES

My search resulted in eight Principles of Family that are consonant with democratic values. Each focuses on the individual members of a system. Any group of people who work together and share the resources and consequences of their activities form a family system. While the principles can apply to a classroom, school, business or community, the present focus is on the nuclear or extended family, your family.

I have worded each principle to emphasize the dual role of rights (receiver) and responsibilities (provider). You take the responsibility perspective when you ask, "How do my actions help others access the rights identified in the principles?" You take the rights perspective when you ask, "What can others do to allow me access to the rights indicated in the principles?" You need to consider both perspectives.

The following presents the principles and gives a few comments on each and their interrelationship. Later chapters embellish on them, and the appendix includes the principles as a poster.

> **1. Principle of Health.** Family members have the right to emotional, intellectual and physical health, and the responsibility to promote the same for others.

The promotion of physical health depends on our knowledge in areas of medicine, nutrition, exercise and stress management. Promoting emotional and intellectual health has a lot to do with how we feel about ourselves and our knowledge of how capable we are at learning about, managing and performing the activities we face. In other words, our emotional and intellectual health is often dependent on our self-management and self-knowledge, as well as our activity skills. If we are sick, injured, or can't complete our activities, our emotional health can be impaired. The three forms of health are interdependent.

2. **Principle of Representation.**   Family members have the right to speak out about the design and implementation of their family activities, and the responsibility to promote the same for others.

The principle of representation notes that members have the right to speak out, as well as the responsibility to make sure that everyone has been heard from. Today when people represent themselves, we praise their assertiveness. When managers promote representation, we admire their commitment to shared leadership and participative management.

3. **Principle of Justice.**   Family members have the right to impartial judgment in conflicts, and the responsibility to promote the same for others.

When family members have different ideas, conflicts can arise. The principle of justice provides a process to insure that family members resolve their conflicts and keep moving forward on their tasks. By teaching ourselves to intervene in our own conflicts—a self-management strategy—we increase our chances of representation and justice.

4. **Principle of Membership.**   Family members have the right to the participation and cooperation of one another, and the responsibility to provide the same for others.

The principle of membership gives a person the right to the support of his family members for any activity that doesn't violate the Principles of Family, and cites the responsibility to provide that support to others. Helping and sharing—two other self-management strategies—are ways of participating and cooperating.

Sometimes an activity is not something another family member wants that person to undertake. For example, a father may want his son to play football, and the son may want to play the piano instead. The son's choice, even though it conflicts with his father's representation, should be supported by the father. The father may not be able to teach piano, but he can help his son get to the lessons and encourage him at times of need. The greatest reason for allowing the choice is that it doesn't break any of the Principles of Family.

5. Principle of Quality.   Family members have the right to perform their tasks at a level of excellence, and the responsibility to promote the same for others.

When the service or product of a task creates the consequences that the family desires, quality has been achieved. These consequences may be aesthetic as well as functional. To promote quality, the family has the responsibility to provide the necessary resources and training when possible, and to understand that the definition of quality changes over time. The criteria used to assess a child's performance in achieving excellence are not the same as they are for an adult.

6. Principle of Adaptation.   Family members have the right to change so they can handle existing activities, and the responsibility to help others do so.

The principle of adaptation asserts that members have the right to function competently across the widest possible range of family activities. With adaptation, family members develop a sense of responsibility for one another and confidence in their ability to perform necessary activities. As an outcome, any family member, during times of need or crisis, will be able to take over the activities of others. The principle of adaptation is an extension of the principles of membership and quality. It adds flexibility to the family and moves toward eliminating discrimination on the basis of age and gender. Overall, members will have fewer expectations about who should perform what types of tasks.

7. Principle of Evolution.   Family members have the right to change so they can function in a wider range of activities and systems, and the responsibility to help others do so.

As the world around the family evolves, the family must do the same. The principle of evolution focuses on insuring adaptation to change. The son in the above example may be the first musical person in the family. The principle of evolution allows for experimentation and individual expression within and outside an existing family system.

Adapting and evolving, principles six and seven, can create a tension. To adapt to existing activities may require conformity to tradition, and to evolve may require a break from it. But to work toward all the Principles of Family will often counter potential conflicts between the principles of adaptation and evolution.

> **8. Principle of Conservation**. Family members have the right to conserve resources so that present and future systems have an increased chance to function according to the Principles of Family, and the responsibility for helping others do so.

The principle of conservation reminds us that families are not alone, and that we have an obligation to future generations and to the planet itself not to waste or over-consume our resources.

WHY THESE PRINCIPLES?

Should there be more? What about equality, humility, patience, honesty, compassion, and forgiveness, to name just a few? I believe that the answer is that equality, humility and the others are *features* of following the eight Principles of Family. By giving energy to all eight principles, you contribute to the equilibrium and growth of the individual and the family. In so doing, you will see the features emerge the way sound does as water passes over rocks in a brook. The principles form a system. You can consider each of them in every human activity.

When you contribute to someone the training needed to adapt, you are promoting his or her equality. When you allow others to represent themselves and provide them with membership, you are showing patience and compassion. The father's acceptance in the above example of representation and membership illustrates an instance of humility and forgiveness. By taking on the responsibility side of the Principles of Family, the more these features emerge.

There is another reason for these principles. If your behaviors are congruent with the Principles of Family, you help create a democratic society. As your children enter other systems, they will work toward the same ends. When we are rewarded for what we create, we come to value both the actions that create and the creation. If we are rewarded for following the Principles of Family, they will become that which we value. They are democratic values in the broadest sense.

Imagine that you have successfully taught your family to manage themselves and follow the Principles of Family. You would see cooperation, participative planning, shared leadership, and adaptation to the changes that every family faces. These are the things that bring families closer together—they work for each other, they do things with each other, they help each other define and reach their goals. In the meantime, you can partake in the daily becoming of your evolving children. The more you understand self-management, the more you can enjoy their evolution and the success of your efforts.

CHAPTER 3

ANALYZING FAMILY ACTIVITIES

It is within your family's activities that you and your children learn to manage yourselves. Clearly analyzed activities help you to move through your days with motivation. You know what needs to be done and why. Chapter 10 will show you how to use the planning strategy to design and evaluate new activities. But first, let's look at existing ones.

Family activities can be divided into three useful categories: regular, project, and special. *Regular activities* are those in which you participate consistently. They cycle in and out of your life on a daily, weekly, monthly, or even yearly basis. You get ready for work, wash clothes, make dinner, work, exercise, play cards with friends, or watch a movie on a daily or weekly schedule. You pay bills, vacation, service the car, and clean the garage monthly or yearly. Some regular activities, like mowing the lawn or shoveling snow, can be thought of as seasonal.

Project activities form the second type. These activities may take a few days or years to complete, and often are composed of many smaller activities. Usually, you work on these projects in your spare time. Examples include learning a new computer software application, remodeling the kitchen, teaching a child to read, or going to college part time.

Special activities form the third type. They can occur at any point during regular or project activities. A sudden change in conditions sets the occasion for these activities. At work, home or school, we often need to get a resource, get help, stop a conflict, protect ourselves from danger, or provide aid to someone. Planning for special activities helps increase the probability that your family will adapt to whatever sudden changes it faces.

I recommend two activities for all families. The first is group planning. By planning for changes, you help insure equilibrium and adaptation. Additionally, your family's planning activity provides an opportunity to teach and learn about self-management and the Principles of Family. Chapter 10 outlines family activity planning. The second recommended activity is a teaching activity. You begin teaching your children with walking, dressing and talking. By setting aside a few minutes each day to teach your children self-management skills, you add to their adaptation and evolution.

LISTING ACTIVITIES

Make a list of your family's activities. All family members old enough to do so may participate. List the activities in the three activity groups: regular, project and special. Next to each regular and project activity, indicate how often it is done—whether daily, weekly, monthly or yearly. There is no need for exactness. The goal is to get a general picture of your activities and how often they are done. For now, just having listed them is enough.

You should see a great deal of similarity in your family members' lives. For most of us, the weekdays are routine. Only a few hours a day and the weekend break the routine. Evenings and weekends provide extra time for the regular activities of recreation, house maintenance, or for one of the project activities. Interruptions to this routine often require you to use special activities.

PARTS OF AN ACTIVITY

Knowing the components of an activity helps you to do a better job of both analyzing and planning them. Every activity has three parts: conditions, behaviors, and consequences.

Conditions

Conditions make an activity possible. They include things like tools, materials, the people involved, and the time and space available. These are often called resources. Yet conditions are more than resources. There are those things like the weather, a birth in the family, your age or health, and the conflicts that family systems experience that impact what activity you perform and how you perform it.

Behaviors

The second part of an activity is behavior, or what you actually do. Often we use the words behavior, actions and skills synonymously. Your behaviors react to or utilize the available conditions so that the activity can be completed and its problems solved. While some conditions are beyond your control, the quality of your life is dependent upon your ability to respond appropriately to them as they arise. Several types of skills help you handle both the activities you plan and those which are thrust on you.

The first is *task behavior.* It achieves the objective of the activity. Reading is the task behavior of a "reading a book" activity; running or calisthenics may be the task behavior of an "exercise" activity; and going on a date may be part of a "courtship" activity.

Self-management behavior manages task behavior during an activity. For example, to manage a "reading a book" activity, your daughter must locate some books, select one, go to a place to read, open the book, turn pages, and return the book when she finishes. None of these behaviors are the "reading" task behavior. But all of them help it begin, continue and end the behavior.

For such simple activities as reading a book and washing the dishes, you do the self-management behaviors without thinking. But when faced with new or complex activities, especially those involving others, you need to use the strategies. When working alone, you might think of them as self-control, self-reliance, or self-discipline. When working with others, they are often called interpersonal skills. When the task contains problems, self-management becomes problem-solving and decision-making.

You and your children need one other type of behavior: *self-knowledge.* Inappropriate self-knowledge can reduce or eliminate your chances of success. If you or your children don't believe that the activity can be done, it may not even start. If you or they take on inappropriate activities, the result will be delay, if not costly failure. Fortunately, you and your children can gain accurate, positive self-knowledge by learning self-management skills, because they help you to describe and predict such things as the plans that must be made, what needs to be learned, what you can or can't do, the consequences of an activity, and the extent to which you value your behavior, the activity, and its consequences. Knowing such things is a large and important part of self-knowledge. It encompasses self-esteem and self-concept. In later chapters, I will illustrate how to promote accurate self-knowledge.

The triangle-shaped figure illustrates the relationship among the three types of activity behavior. Task behavior actually performs the activity task (center triangle). Self-management and self-knowledge provide support for it and, in turn, support each other. If any one of these three behaviors is weak or inappropriate, you reduce your chances of performing the activity successfully and producing the desired consequences.

ACTIVITY BEHAVIORS
———— Within Any Task/Problem Activity ————

TASK BEHAVIORS

ACTIVITY PERFORMANCE

SELF-MANAGEMENT BEHAVIORS

SELF-KNOWLEDGE BEHAVIORS

Consequences

Your handling of the conditions of an activity produces consequences. Often we talk of consequences as results or outcomes. Essentially, they mean the same thing. When you build a chair, you can sit on it and relax. NASA went to the moon and was able to study it in new ways. You correctly balance your checkbook and know how much money you have for something you would like to do. These changes can have an impact on both you and others. The chair can be sat on by others, we all know more about the moon, and the new activity may involve the whole family.

Consequences reinforce or punish behavior. As a result, the behavior will change in the sense of increase or decrease in the future. This is the power of consequences. If the family and school environment reinforces a child's poem writing, it will increase over time. If the environment punishes poem writing, it will decrease over time and cease. If the environment both reinforces and punishes the poem writing, it will vacillate, as will the emotions of the child.

Individuals provide reciprocal consequences for each other. The parent teaches the child to read. The reading reinforces the parent, and the parent in turn reinforces the child with praise and access to other activities. Both the reading and teaching will increase, as will many behaviors connected to learning, parenting and relating. Family members influence and are influenced by one another. This mutual relationship promotes the coherence, adaptation and survival of the family. Children and parents come to trust each other. Each can lead or follow when needed.

Consequences take three forms. Restructuring consequences are physical or behavioral changes in the world. Teaching children to read changes them into readers. Washing dishes ends in clean dishes. Building produces a home. Making love can conceive a child. An accident causes injury.

Another form of consequence is access to events. When children can read, they can read to themselves, and parents can access other activities. The dishes are available for the next meal. The home can be lived in. The new baby accesses life. The injury may require medical care.

Consequences can also be emotional. Although our language of these internal consequences is approximate at best, we all understand the "wow" of a backflip, the exhilaration of solving a problem, the high from exercise, the pride from building a home, the rush and relaxation of making love, and the contentment from a fine day's work. These are the positive emotional consequences. We also understand the negative, or punishing, ones: the pain from a backflip done wrong, the frustration from a problem not solved, the anxiety and fear that can accompany making love, and the stress that comes from an excessive day's work.

Restructuring, access, and emotional consequences often occur closely in time, with each contributing to reinforcing or punishing behavior for the individual or others. For example, getting dressed changes the dresser, allows her access to places that require clothes, and can make her feel good. Making love can be emotionally fulfilling, conceive a child, and provide further access to conversation, intimacy, or sleep.

As you and your children grow, consequences gain or lose power. They evolve. Yet much commonality remains. Throughout our lives, hugs, kisses, caresses, laughs, smiles and kind words continue to reinforce us all.

Relationship of Activity Parts

The conditions, behaviors and consequences of an activity are in relationship with one another. These relationships are contingent, or "if/then" conditionals. If you behave in particular ways under particular conditions, then particular consequences will occur. For example, with water, soap, dirty dishes, and sink (conditions), you wash and dry (behavior), so you have clean dishes, a chance to eat off them, and avoid getting sick (consequences). If you lacked soap, you would have to change your behavior; and if you had no dirty dishes, you would not "do the dishes." *Activity contingencies* range from the simple, like dishwashing, to the complex, like building a house or going to the moon.

The figure on the facing page gives a picture of an activity as a contingency. The direction of the arrows indicates that it is the behavior that takes conditions and produces consequences. When your behavior can handle the conditions, desirable consequences usually occur. The dishes are washed, the moon is reached, the account is balanced.

Part of the behavior of handling the activity contingency is learning what consequences spring from particular condition-behavior relationships, which I have indicated by the box around the conditions and behaviors in the figure. Our present concern for the environment and the economic plight of our nation arises from an understanding of real or potential consequences that occur because of condition-behavior relationships. If you don't understand what consequences your behavior produces, you can endanger yourself and others. In other words, conditions and consequences will handle you and your future behavior instead of the other way around.

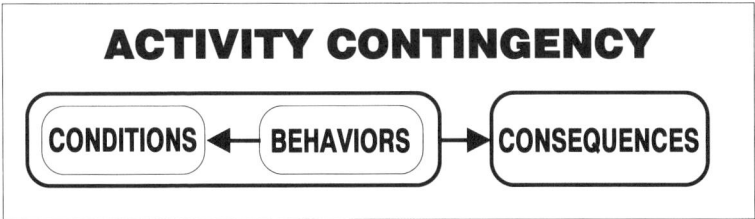

ACTIVITY CONTINGENCY

CONDITIONS ← BEHAVIORS → CONSEQUENCES

ANALYZING ACTIVITY PARTS

Next, open each family activity and identify the activity contingency needed for its completion. You may think many activities are so simple that they do not need to be analyzed. The activity contingency is obvious. You know the resources available, how to manage and perform the activity, and what happens as a result. Your children's understanding is a different matter. They do not know the conditions, the behaviors, or the consequences. You will need to teach them. A careful analysis of activities can insure success.

Children's first activities include eating, drinking, dressing, and using the potty. Along the way they learn to walk and talk. Later, they participate in any number of family activities like washing dishes, feeding pets, making beds, and mowing the lawn. You will need to teach these. Once your children learn some of the basic individual and family tasks, you begin teaching the self-management strategies.

Analyzing activities is just as important for adult family members. Whenever you do something that involves others or is highly complex, the analysis of that activity is necessary to insure the desired consequences. How-to books, instructional videos, or community college classes can help you gain the necessary task skills, but you will have to provide the self-management to get the job done. The following sections show you how to analyze an activity into its conditions, behaviors and consequences.

Analyzing Behaviors

Choose an activity from your list. What behaviors are required? Many conflicts occur because the behaviors of an activity are not clear. These are the "you-should-have-done" and "look-what-you-forgot" conflicts that many families experience. Use the following simple procedure to eliminate these conflicts. The procedure has four steps.

1. Identify the major task and self-management behaviors.
2. Identify the behaviors needing further analysis.
3. Break those down into easy-to-follow steps.
4. List the steps that each family member does.

Step 1. Start by walking through the activity as if you were going to do it yourself. This makes the analysis manageable. Let's look at getting dressed, one of the first activities your children will need to learn. Here are the major task behaviors a little boy might need for getting dressed.

1. Put on undershorts.
2. Put on undershirt.
3. Put on shirt.
4. Button shirt.*
5. Put on pants.
6. Zip up pants.*
7. Put on belt.
8. Buckle belt.*
9. Put on socks.
10. Put on shoes.
11. Tie shoes.*

The major self-management behaviors he would need for these dressing behaviors are planning, organizing and supervising.

Step 2. A behavior needs further analysis when it can't be displayed in a second or two or requires some fine movements that those who are learning may not have mastered. Of all the task behaviors, only four of the eleven need further analysis. They are marked with stars in the above list. All the self-management behaviors need further analysis.

Step 3. This time you walk through each of the identified behaviors. Of the four task behaviors, tying shoes (11) is the most complex. Here are its behaviors.

1. Pull laces tight.
2. Put one lace over and under the other lace.
3. Pull laces tight.
4. Holding tight, make loop with one lace.
5. Put other lace over and under the first lace.
6. Grasp the top of loop and the other lace where it goes under.
7. Pull both laces tight.

Each of these behavioral steps can now be modeled in a second. They form a little procedure. Almost everything that requires further analysis is a procedure. The task behaviors of buckling, buttoning and zipping are procedures with fewer parts, but they also consist of fine motor movements that could initially give the child a problem. Thus, they need further analysis. When you can easily model, or show, all the pieces of a behavior, it can be easily taught and learned.

Finding the self-management behaviors is a little different. This time you walk through the strategy steps. The daily planning for dressing includes deciding what needs to be worn (strategy step 1, identify the problem). Knowledge of the weather and the day's activities control this decision. The organizing self-management behaviors include identifying the clothes to be worn (step 1, identify resources), locating where they were washed and ironed (step 2, locate resources), transferring them to the place where dressing is done (step 3, transfer resources), and arranging them for dressing (step 4, arrange resources). The last step would include putting them in a chest or closet when clean, or in the hamper if dirty. The supervision behavior primarily focuses on identifying when to be dressed (step 2, tell about the plan), directing the order in which clothes are put on (step 4, directing task flow), and looking to see that everything is on correctly (step 5, look for success).

The self-management behaviors could be expanded to cover planning and organizing a wardrobe in the sense of deciding what is needed and shopping for it. You treat these as other activities because of their distance in time and place from the immediate dressing.

Step 4. Take note of who does what parts of the activity. Some family activities are primarily done by an individual, some are done by groups, and some can be done either way. Since the family principle of membership focuses on cooperation, you will want to plan activities so that your children have a chance to work regularly with you or their siblings. Activities like dishwashing, car care, house cleaning and lawn work are a few that you can do alone but offer a great opportunity for developing the cooperative attribute of self-management behavior. Moreover, virtually all activities are learned first by doing them together. Gradually, you turn a greater share over to your children.

Now return to your list of activities, and perform the above analysis for a few of the activities that are of interest to you. Note the major task and self-management behaviors and who does what parts. As a parent, you should do this for activities your children are about to enter and in which they are already participating.

Analyzing Conditions

Conditions consist primarily of resources, like the persons working on the task, the available tools, the materials and time needed, and the place to do the task. To identify resources, you walk through the activity again. Just follow the behaviors, noting the resources involved and the time it takes to complete the activity. Children usually dress in the bedroom, in the morning, and with the identified clothes. The room contains a dresser, closet, chair and bed. If the child is younger than three, she may need some assistance getting dressed. Therefore, a parent or sibling is needed. That is all there is to it.

Analyzing Consequences

You can identify the consequences of an activity by answering a set of questions.

1. Who is affected by the activity?
2. What are the consequences for each of them?
3. Are any consequences returned (reciprocated)?
4. What will be the effect of these consequences on future behavior?

The answers give you a good idea about the range and power of each activity's consequences. For the dressing example, the child and the parents are the most affected. The child is dressed and gains access to an array of events and praise from parents (especially when the behavior is new). When the child can dress herself, the parents gain time for other activities. When she can do the self-management elements of dressing, the parents' and the child's freedom increase even more. These consequences are positive.

The emotion felt by parents and child will depend on the way in which they see dressing. If the child sees that her behavior does something for the parents, dressing will be emotionally reinforced. If the parents see the dressing as an indication of progress toward a self-managed child, they will be emotionally reinforced. But if they see it as "she finally learned to dress herself," they will find no delight. The child is gaining self-knowledge, and the parents' perspective helps create it.

As children grow older and take on family-based activities, the analysis of consequences stays pretty much the same. Let's say that your son is now doing the dishes most evenings. He "may not mind" doing them, and his getting an allowance may be contingent on it. The whole family is going to benefit from clean dishes. You feel good that your son is doing the dishes; you have access to other activities. You can reciprocally reinforce your son by thanking him. And with the extra time you have, you can even enjoy some event together.

The extent to which consequences are rewarding for the family depends on your skill at seeing them and teaching your children to see them as well. With the analysis of activity consequences, you have completed a good first look at the contingencies of your family's activities.

TWO SPECIAL NOTES

First, as your children develop, new activities emerge. Children go down and across the street, go to school, see movies, stay overnight with friends, and drive to distant places. As these activities emerge, you move from the analysis of activities to planning them. As you plan with your children, you do one important thing different from the above analysis. You establish, not just discover, consequences.

Most of these allow them access to a larger world. If the child wants to go to the movies with a friend, he should be able to tell you the plan, and the two of you agree on the consequences of following and not following the plan. If the child says he will be home by 9:00 p.m. and is not, what consequences will occur? If he is late, do you both think it would be fair that he stays home for the next week? This process is called establishing contingent consequences. What happens is contingent on the child's behavior. Now reverse the picture. What happens if you plan with your child, and you don't carry out your end? Should you stay home? The rights and responsibilities expressed in the Principles of Family are not just for children.

Not everything is negotiable, but most activities include choices. Whether to have vegetables with dinner may not be negotiable, for instance, but children should have a choice between this or that vegetable when possible. These choices are the child's first contributions to the family's plans. How to go about planning and establishing consequences is covered in almost every chapter that remains in this book.

Second, when parents manage their own and their children's regular activities, there is little time left for them to relax or renew themselves. All parents get more than a little tired of changing diapers, feeding and dressing children. Yet many parents keep planning, organizing and supervising even after their children can dress, toilet, and feed themselves. Why? Because the children have not learned the self-management skills that are a part of these activities. They can get dressed by themselves, but they can't wash and iron their own clothes or even get them into the hamper. They can eat, but they can't set the table, make breakfast, or clean up after themselves. They can comb their hair and shower, but they leave the bathroom a mess. Guess who does all the rest?

Teaching your children to manage themselves means that they can contribute to the performance and management of family activities. As a consequence, you have a different sort of relationship with them—one that keeps you vital through the curiosity, energy and growth they model. To gain that, you must do two things. The first is to analyze the task and self-management behaviors and consequences of family activities. The second is to teach them to perform and manage those and the new activities that occur because of their growth.

CHAPTER 4

TEACHING

There are at least five good reasons why you can teach your children self-management skills. First, you already know something about the components of self-management. Second, your family is a perfect teaching environment. Third, children learn a little at a time, so you don't have to be an expert before you start teaching. Fourth, the pattern of teaching is virtually the same for any behavior that needs to be taught. And fifth, I will give you the tools to insure your success. The language of self-management, the ways of teaching, and how to arrange teaching in your family system may be new to you; but with the support I give, they will become second nature. You will know what to do, and your children will know what to expect.

THE TOOLS OF TEACHING

The teacher first asks, "How can I establish conditions and consequences so that some piece of useful behavior occurs?" The tools of teaching identify the possibilities.

Condition Tools

Condition tools set the occasion for behavior in three ways: modeling, prompting, and testing.

The Modeling Tool. The first is to *model*, or demonstrate, the behavior to be learned. The learner watches the model. The model can be both a physical demonstration and a verbal one. For you, the adult reader, Chapter 1 modeled the self-management strategies and their relationship. It did all that in a few pages that included figures and several examples. But when you teach your child, you will want to model little pieces of self-management behavior at a time.

The Prompting Tool. The *prompt* supports behavior. After the model, the learner usually needs some help. There are two basic types of prompts. First, prompts are physical guides. Examples include holding your child's hand with a spoon in it and moving it toward her mouth, using training wheels on a bicycle, or indicating with a nod or a hand movement when something should happen. Second, prompts can be verbal guides in the sense of helping someone say a new word, telling him when to start or stop, what to look for, or asking what part of behavior comes next. These verbal prompts can be written or spoken. When spoken, we often call them "hints." You will use the posters of the self-management strategies presented in Chapters 6 through 12 as prompts.

Because learners need to perform independently, you remove prompts as soon as possible, but often in steps. You provide each step, or stage, until the child can perform successfully several times, then remove the prompt or use less of it. To remove a prompt is to "fade" it. You raise the training wheels on the bicycle before removing them. You take down the poster of the strategy and replace it with a verbal prompt like, "What strategy can you use now?" or "What strategy step is next?" Eventually even these can be dropped.

For very complex behavior, or where the consequences could be harmful, prompts are continually used. NASA astronauts and ground crews follow checklists, as do airline pilots and deep-sea divers. For complex self-management behavior, especially in groups, keep the posters up for everyone to see.

The Testing Tool. A *test* minimally sets the occasion for behavior. When you have faded the prompt, the test has arrived. You test to determine whether the learner can perform independently. For you, this book can't test your knowledge about, or your knowledge of how, to perform self-management; but it does show you how to evaluate your success.

Consequence Tools

During instruction, learners—children or adults—behave in two ways: managing themselves (usually called paying attention and following instructions) and demonstrating that they have learned. You positively reinforce these behaviors to increase their future probability. The kiss, hug, pat, smile, laugh, and good words are all consequences that reinforce the learner during or after teaching. For the child, you initially associate physical contact and good words, which give the words extra power. Additionally, use your words to pinpoint the accuracy and consistency of what was produced, as well as the access and emotional consequences for the learner and others.

The next figure illustrates the pattern that is followed in using the tools of teaching. It is this pattern that helps make teaching manageable. You begin with models, move to prompts when necessary, test, and use reinforcing consequences all along the way. The model demonstrates behavior. The prompt supports behavior. The test provides the learner with an opportunity to show he has become independent, that he has learned. And reinforcing consequences increase the probability that the behavior will continue into the future and be cemented to conditions. This is the pattern you follow in using the tools of teaching.

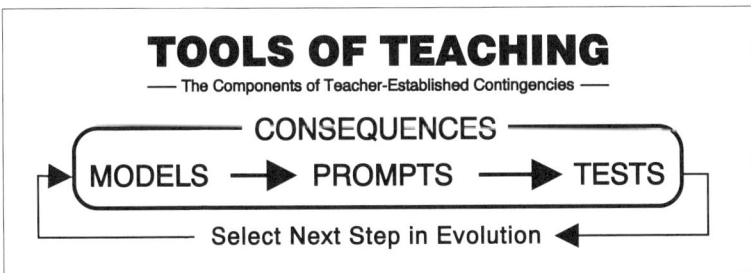

TOOLS OF TEACHING
—— The Components of Teacher-Established Contingencies ——
CONSEQUENCES
MODELS → PROMPTS → TESTS
Select Next Step in Evolution ◄

PROCEDURES OF TEACHING

With the tools of teaching in hand, the teacher can ask the second question of teaching: "How can I transform a fledgling learner into one who is highly skilled?" You don't just put a new pilot into the cockpit of a 747, nor do you give the management of government over to those who have no experience. The same is true for self-management behavior. It evolves.

For each type of evolution, you use a procedure of teaching. Find a middle ground in its use that provides enough challenge, yet results in success most of the time. I have kept the teaching procedures to a minimum so that you and your children can focus on what is being taught and not on how it is being taught.

Initial Teaching

When a behavior *emerges*, it comes to life for the first time. Fred says his first word, Tony uses the potty chair for the first time, Rhoda organizes her first activity, or Wendy identifies something as a conflict. Teaching that causes behavior to emerge is called *initial teaching*. An initial teaching procedure can use all the tools of teaching.

For example, you will want to teach your child knowledge about conflicts. To do that, you first model by mixing multiple examples and non-examples to show the range and limits of what a conflict is. Many different types of interactions are conflicts (their range), while others might be confused with conflicts (their limits). During teaching, you put together three to six examples and non-examples, one after the other, to model. The following example illustrates a parent modeling conflict identification for a child about four years of age.

> PARENT: Let me show you what a conflict is. A conflict stops activities. Here's an example. You and Mike push each other to use the train set. That's a conflict.
> PARENT: Next. You and Marshall play with the train set together, taking turns driving and loading the cars. That's not a conflict.
> PARENT: Next. You don't put your clothes away like I ask. Conflict or not a conflict? Conflict.
> PARENT: Next. Marshall doesn't come to dinner when asked. Conflict or not a conflict? Conflict.
> PARENT: Next. Marshall asks me if he can help me set the table for dinner. Conflict or not a conflict? Not a conflict.

These five examples modeled conflicts and non-conflicts. It did so within the context of what the child already knew—her brother, parent, setting the table, toys, pushing, shoving, and coming to dinner. Examples one and two show limits, as do four and five. They are much alike, but are responded to differently. Examples one, three, and four illustrate a range of what constitutes a conflict. The parent responded to them in the same way. You could arrange this set differently as long as it showed range and limits.

Immediately, you follow the above models with a set of tests that include similar examples and non-examples. Here is a sample.

PARENT: **I liked the way you listened. Your turn.** You and Mike work together to clean up the toys before dinner. Conflict or not a conflict?

ZELDA: Not a conflict.

PARENT: **That's it. Next.** I wash the dishes and you wipe. Conflict or not a conflict?

ZELDA: Not a conflict.

PARENT: **Next.** You put your clothes in the hamper when they are dirty. Conflict or not a conflict?

ZELDA: Not a conflict.

PARENT: **Correct. [Parent hugs Zelda.] Next.** You don't answer me when I ask you a question. Conflict or not a conflict?

ZELDA: Conflict.

PARENT: **Great. You know about conflicts.**

These tests consist of examples and non-examples that covered about the same range and limits as the models.

For an isolated piece of knowledge like what a conflict is, only models, tests and consequences may need to be used. The consequences were in **bold** type. The first came as the parent transitioned from models to tests, "I like the way you listened. Your turn." This reinforced attending to the models directly and indicated access to the tests. The others indicate the child was correct, and all the "Next" statements indicate access to the next example because of success. You will use such presentation formats to teach a number of bits of knowledge about self-management.

But you can't always teach such an isolated piece of knowledge, like what constitutes a conflict. This is especially true when you teach your children the individual self-management strategies. You will be teaching them knowledge about the steps of a strategy (including the vocabulary) and how to perform them at the same time. Here, you can't use multiple models. Instead you model each step of the strategy, giving it a name. To stay within the knowledge base of the child, you model the strategy within a well known activity in which both you and your child have participated. She learns to see the activity as having parts and can follow this model because she is familiar with the activity. You model each step, or part, of the strategy and verbally point out what you are doing as you move from one step to the next. The following example illustrates a parent modeling the organizing strategy for a child about four years old. The strategy name and steps are indicated in **bold**.

PARENT: Let's **organize** for our "reading together" activity. First, we **identify what we need**. We need a good place to sit, and what else?
ZELDA: A book.
PARENT: Excellent. So we have identified what we need. Second, we must **locate** what we need. We can sit over there. Where is a book?
ZELDA: [Points to books.]
PARENT: Third, we **transfer** ourselves so we can read. Can you get the book and go over to the couch?
ZELDA: Yes. [Gets book and goes to couch.]
PARENT: Fourth, we **arrange** ourselves. Do you want to sit on my lap?
ZELDA: Yes.
PARENT: So let's read. [Reads and interacts with Zelda.] Now for the last part of organizing. We finish arranging by **returning** everything we used. Can you put the book back?
ZELDA: Yes. [Returns book.]
PARENT: See how easy **organizing** is. Will you be ready to organize with me tomorrow?
ZELDA: Yes.

The parent clearly laid out the vocabulary of organizing and modeled the steps for an activity that the child and parent had performed together in the past. The parent had been doing the organizing and did so again in the model. Yet the child participated to some extent in each step of the strategy.

With the teaching of the procedures and language of the self-management strategies, you will use many prompts to move the child from model to test. The following example illustrates prompting during one of the early interactions following the above model. The prompts are in **bold**. The reinforcing consequences are in *italics*.

PARENT: Zelda, can you organize us for our reading time and tell me about it as you do?

ZELDA: Yes. First, I identify that we need a book and a place to sit down.

PARENT: **What is the next step of organizing?**

ZELDA: I find what we need. [Points to books and couch.]

PARENT: **What do organizers call "finding what you need?"**

ZELDA: I don't remember.

PARENT: Locate. You locate what you need. **Can you say it?**

ZELDA: I locate the books and couch.

PARENT: *Okay.* **You have located, and what is next?**

ZELDA: I remember this one! We transfer to the couch with the book. [Gets book and moves to couch.]

PARENT: *Yes. [Moves to couch.]*

ZELDA: Last, we arrange ourselves on the couch. You sit here, and I sit here and hold the book.

PARENT: *I thought the arrange step would trip you up. You fooled me. [Reads and interacts with Zelda.] Well, that was a funny story.* **What is the very last part of arranging?**

ZELDA: I return the book?

PARENT: *Yes, returning the book is the very last part of organizing. You are certainly beginning to get the steps of organizing.* **What step gave you trouble this time?**

ZELDA: Locating. But I knew what to do.

PARENT: **I also know you will get locating right the next time.** *[Big hug.] I like reading with you.*

Gradually, you fade, or remove, the prompts until the child can name the steps of organizing and do the organizing for the activity. Learning the correct words for the steps helps the child to apply the strategy across a wider range of activities, as described in the following section on expansion teaching.

In the following example, the child passes a test. The parts of the test are in **bold**. The consequences are in *italics*.

PARENT: Zelda, can you organize us for our reading time and tell me about it as you do?

ZELDA: Yes. First, I identify that we need a book and a place to sit down. They are located there and there. [Points.] Next, we transfer to the couch. Would you get the book on the way?

PARENT: *Yes. [Gets book and moves to couch.]*

ZELDA: Last, we arrange ourselves on the couch. You sit here, and I sit here and hold the book.

PARENT: *[Reads and interacts with Zelda.]* We have finished the story. **What now?**

ZELDA: I return the book to finish organizing for reading time.

PARENT: *That's it! That's the first time you got all the organizing words right as you organized us. You're really getting those words that help us work together. [Big hug.]*

The parent's teaching began by providing Zelda with the opportunity to match description with organizing action. It became a test because no prompts were needed. Zelda named the parts of organizing and carried it out. Moving from the modeling interaction to this test would take about four to seven interactions over as many days for a four year old. The initial teaching for "conflict" took only one interaction and about two minutes, and may need to be repeated on the next day. Both of these teaching interactions could have been done during the family teaching activity mentioned in Chapter 3, but the teaching of organizing could as easily have been performed during the reading activity.

To increase your knowledge of the strategies, I suggest you put up a copy of the self-management poster presented in the appendix in a place that is convenient for review, such as the kitchen or bathroom. The poster combines the figures presented in Chapter 1. Each morning try to remember the steps and elements of one or more strategies. Every once in a while, sit down and try to reproduce these figures on paper. For most adults, that only takes about two weeks if they work at it a few minutes a day.

Expansion Teaching

Initial teaching gets behavior going under very restricted conditions, but once emerged, it continues to evolve. *Expansion teaching* insures that behavior 1) occurs across a wide range of activities, and 2) is successful within any of them. It makes the behavior applicable, adaptable, and flexible. Most expansion teaching for the self-management strategies is done with four procedures: teaching the strategy across familiar activities, employing the What Management Game, teaching the strategy elements, and using family activity planning.

Teaching the Strategy Across Familiar Activities. Following initial teaching, you want your children to begin to use the strategy across a range of activities in which they already participate. Here is an example.

> PARENT: Now that you can organize and tell me the steps for our reading activity, you can begin to do it for all your other activities as well. Let's do it for changing the bedding. First you identify that we need to change the bedding. What do we need?
> ZELDA: We need sheets and pillow cases.
> PARENT: Those are the resources we need. What step of organizing is next?
> ZELDA: I locate the resources. They are in the closet.
> PARENT: What's the third step of organizing?
> ZELDA: Transfer. We go to the closet and get some sheets and pillow cases. [Goes and gets resources with parent.]
> PARENT: Okay, what's next?
> ZELDA: We arrange them on the chair so we can get the sheets first and then the pillow cases. Now we change the bedding. [Changes bedding with parent.]
> PARENT: What is the last thing we do?
> ZELDA: We take the old sheets and pillow cases to the hamper.
> PARENT: That's all there is to organizing for changing the bedding. You got all the steps right the first time. And it only took a few seconds to finish the task. Great organizing and team work. Thank you. [Hug.]

The parent prompts Zelda as little as possible, but provides reinforcing consequences as the activity unfolds. For the next activity, you would try to drop as many of the "What's next?" questions as possible. If the child gets stuck, prompt. Usually, reminding the child of a strategy step is enough. Go over each activity until she gets all the strategy steps correct. After about the third activity, she will do it completely by herself the first time you ask. A little later she will begin to tell you about organizing an activity without your asking, or ask about how to organize an activity she is going to do. From this point, the start of an activity will set the occasion for any strategy that has undergone such an expansion.

What Management Game. This game helps insure that the child sees a range of activities in which the strategy applies. It is designed to be fun and can take many forms. Here is a very restricted form of the game for identifying conflicts.

PARENT: [Watching TV with child.] My turn to identify conflicts. Remember that conflicts stop the activity. Conflict or non-conflict? [Points.] It is a conflict. Your turn to identify conflicts. [Points.] Is that a conflict or non-conflict?
ZELDA: It is a conflict.
PARENT: That's it. [Later.] Is that a conflict or not a conflict? [Points.]
ZELDA: A conflict.
PARENT: I agree. Can you tell me whenever you see a conflict?
ZELDA: Yes.
PARENT: [Prompts child if needed with "Is that a conflict?"]

Such an interaction usually begins soon after initial teaching, contains only one or two models, and then continues for five or six test examples. You can do this during any home activity, at the store, driving, or in almost any situation where examples of what you are looking for occur.

As your child continues to learn, you can change the game to include some of the new things learned.

PARENT: [Watching TV with child.] Let's play the What Management Game. First, I will point something out. You tell me if it is an example of a conflict, helping, or sharing. Then you point something out, and I will tell what it is. Your turn. [Points.] What is that?
ZELDA: Helping.
PARENT: How do you know?
ZELDA: The girl made the boy's job easier.
PARENT: I agree. Your turn to ask me when you see helping, sharing, or conflicts.
ZELDA: What is that? [Points.]
PARENT: Conflict.
ZELDA: How do you know?
PARENT: They stopped their activity.
ZELDA: That's what I think, too. [Continues game for a few more minutes.]

The parent would have first taught helping and sharing before their inclusion. The most general form of question for the What Management Game would be to ask, "How are they managing themselves?" From this game it is easy to move to the child's activities and prompt by asking, "What strategy do you use now?" At the start, you may need to add a little more support, for example, "What strategy do you use now, helping or sharing?" Such interactions include reinforcing consequences for child and parent.

Teaching Strategy Elements. The above expansion procedures emphasize insuring that the right strategy occurs across a range of activities, and that children see a range of applications beyond their present experience. To insure strategy success within any of their present or future activities, you teach the strategy elements. The elements break each strategy step into smaller concrete parts. Using this extra detail increases the chance of successful performance. Here are the elements for the first two steps of organizing.

1. IDENTIFY THE RESOURCES
   a. What resources are needed?
   b. How much of each is needed?
2. LOCATE THE RESOURCES
   a. How can the resources be located?
   b. Where are they located?

Five strategies have elements: organizing, supervising, planning, learning and intervening. Begin teaching strategy elements when your child can read. Posters of the strategies are provided to help you model and prompt. Chapters 6 and 9 through 12 present the strategy elements and how to teach them to your children. The appendix presents the posters again so that you can photocopy them for family use.

Family Activity Planning. After children learn the steps of a strategy, they should be able to use that knowledge to help build personal and family plans. You make this happen by involving the child in family activity planning. As your children learn strategy elements, their involvement should increase even more. This expansion allows children to apply the strategy to activities outside their existing range, and helps insure their success when they do. It is a major teaching procedure for any family. You will have to prompt, test, and provide consequences to insure their participation. Chapter 10 illustrates family activity planning.

Refinement Teaching

New behavior is often on shaky ground. Zelda organizes only some of the time and may need to be prompted often to help or share. *Refinement teaching* insures that a strategy is applied with consistency, accuracy and quickness. You start to refine behavior once expansion teaching is underway. You want to insure that the behavior is performed accurately, with each opportunity (consistency), and as soon as needed (quickness). Knowing these three forms of refinement will help you see how your child's self-management behavior is evolving.

You refine behavior first by prompting it and then by reinforcing its occurrence. To help matters, reinforcing one type of refinement will result in others occurring at the same time. Usually, you will mix refinement teaching with expansion teaching. Here is how easy refinement teaching can be.

> PARENT: Let's see how fast you can organize us for reading today.
> ZELDA: [Organizes and describes it.]
> PARENT: That was fast. We are ready to read; and because you organized so fast, we have more time to read.

The prompt establishes the goal of organizing quickly, and the consequence statement describes that fast organizing gave access to more reading. If the parent's statements and reading are reinforcing, then fast organizing will increase. If the organizing was accurate, accuracy would also have been reinforced at the same time as well.

Refinement takes time and requires patience. Knowing the types of refinement helps your patience, because you can see the small increments of evolution. If you teach your children to see their evolution, they will have the tools to refine their own behavior. For the adult, you use knowledge of the types of refinement in the evaluation of your plans. Are your plans and their implementation becoming more accurate, consistent, and quickly carried out? If so, you know refinement is occurring.

Correction Teaching

Behavior not only comes to life, or emerges, but it also dies, or extinguishes. Behavior stops because we have failed to practice it or because behavior that is more reinforcing has replaced it. Children stop babbling when they can talk, and stop crawling when they can walk. The self-management strategies operate in the same way: they replace non-functional or weaker forms of management behaviors.

Correction teaching extinguishes inappropriate behavior and causes appropriate behavior to emerge. It is the special activity of teaching. You do not want your children to practice inappropriate self-management, and at the same time you want to minimize the punishment of being wrong. Correction teaching does this. It is used only when newly emerged, expanded, or refined behavior has been inappropriately performed or can't be performed. Thus, it is sandwiched into ongoing instruction to stop the errors in learning. For example, if Zelda was not able to say "conflict" within any range of acceptability after your modeling, then you would stop, model the behavior, prompt it, test for it, provide reinforcing consequences, and return to your original teaching. Essentially, correction teaching relies on the heavy use of prompts. In the following case, you are teaching how to perform saying the word. The prompts are in **bold**.

Zelda: [Can't say "conflict."]
PARENT: Let me show you how to say "conflict." [Pause.] **Say it with me. [Pause.] Conflict.**
ZELDA: [With parent.] Conflict.
PARENT: **Good. Let's say it together one more time. [Pause.] Conflict.**
ZELDA: [With parent.] Conflict.
PARENT: You got it. Now all by yourself. Say it.
ZELDA: Conflict.
PARENT: Okay. Now let's learn what a conflict is.

The term is first modeled and then prompted twice with "Say it with me." Did the prompting work? The child's reply to the parent's test indicates it did. If you eliminate the prompt in the above teaching, you move directly from model to test. The more sophisticated the child's vocabulary, the less you will have to use such a correction.

The platform for correcting your own self-management behavior is the planning activity. If a plan was evaluated as something less than successful, you go to the learning strategy, if necessary, and then build a better plan.

The figure on the next page illustrates the procedures of teaching and their relationship. Four distinct procedures cause the evolution of behavior. All of them use models, prompts, tests and consequences—the tools of teaching. Initial teaching brings behavior to life for the first time. It may be a simple behavior, like making a sound, saying a word, or identifying helping, sharing or conflicts. It also may bring to life complex behavior like planning or organizing. Expansion teaching follows initial teaching, and insures that the behavior can be performed across a range of activities and under a wider range of conditions to increase the chance of success in any given activity. The figure depicts these two types of expansions by calling them "expansion across" teaching and "expansion within" teaching. For children, expansions across activities start before expansions within activities. But the strict distinction blurs when using variations of the What Management Game and family activity planning. After expansion teaching is underway, you begin refinement. Refinement teaching helps you and your children manage yourselves with greater accuracy, consistency and quickness. If mistakes occur during initial, expansion or refinement teaching, correction teaching is used to stop mistakes and get the appropriate behavior going as soon as possible. Correction teaching is used only when learning does not seem to occur and teaching needs to be strengthened.

A FINAL NOTE

I have presented a model of teaching. And that it what it is—a model. Like all models it is a guide, not an absolute. It is designed to help you teach effectively and communicate with others when you have problems. The same is true for all the chapters that follow. They model how to teach each of the self-management strategies. You can adapt them, using your ingenuity to make changes to fit your family life. As you think about this chapter and those that follow, remember three points:

PROCEDURES OF TEACHING

——— The Types of Contingencies Teachers Establish to Evolve Behavior ———

INITIAL TEACHING
Bringing a Behavior to Life

EXPANSION ACROSS TEACHING
Insuring Behavior Occurs Across a Range of Activities

EXPANSION WITHIN TEACHING
Insuring Behavior Will Succeed in Any Activity

REFINEMENT TEACHING
Insuring Behavior is Consistent, Accurate and Quick

CORRECTION TEACHING
Used Only When Needed to Revise Unsuccessful Teaching

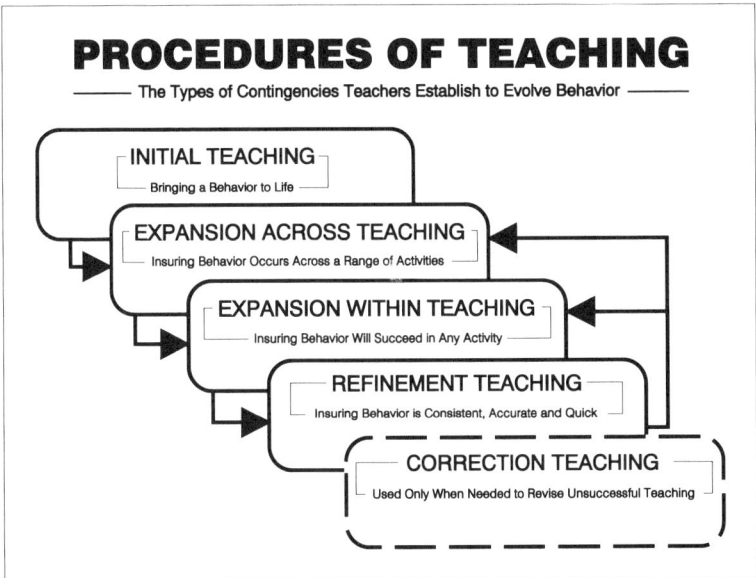

1. There is no perfect way to teach the strategies,
   but there are many effective ones.
2. You can change your teaching plan at any time.
3. Teach so your children love every minute of it.

Most of the models in this book illustrate how to talk to your children. Your words will be different, as will the activities in which you use them. In Chapter 13, I provide guidelines to help you plan your teaching from beginning to end. These guidelines are another model. Adapt it to your needs.

CHAPTER 5

THINKING AHEAD AND BEHIND

Thinking ahead and behind makes it possible to be independent and adaptive. Thinking ahead builds a plan. Thinking behind evaluates it. When you sandwich them together, they form the inductive process. Everyone from the scientist to the corporate manager to the government official uses this process. Yet the crises that trouble our world attest to the fact that many are not proficient at it. Inductive thinking needs to be pervasive, automatic and accurate. It forms the foundation for understanding responsibility and building strong self-management skills. This chapter explores the process of inductive thinking and how to teach it to your children while engaged in your regular, everyday activities with them.

INDUCTIVE THINKING

Thinking ahead and behind are both inductive. Each forms an argument, the conclusion of which goes beyond the evidence or premises. The inductive thinking process has three major components: a prediction argument, observation of changes, and an evaluation argument. Each argument consists of premises and conclusion. The prediction argument presents supporting evidence statements (as premises) and a prediction statement (as conclusion). For example:

P1: Each time I have worn mittens in cold weather,
      my hands keep warm.
P2: Each time I don't wear mittens in cold weather,
      my hands get cold.

C: If I wear my mittens on this cold day,
      I will keep my hands warm.

The conclusion (C), as prediction, goes beyond the premises (P1 and P2). It was based on the past, but not insured by it.

The evaluation argument presents the observation and other evidence statements (as premises) and an evaluation statement (as conclusion). Here is an example of an evaluation argument that could follow the above prediction argument.

P: I wore mittens and my hands did not get cold.

C: My prediction was correct.

In both arguments, the premises, as evidence, support the conclusion. The stronger the support, the more likely the conclusion. The above observational evidence provides exceptionally strong support. To you it is so obvious as to be trivial, but not to the small child. Initially it is not the content that is important, but the thinking process.

Each argument depends on the other. A prediction without an evaluation would be like throwing a ball (prediction) without ever seeing where it went (evaluation). Throwing would never improve. Predictions improve because the evaluation argument becomes a premise for future prediction arguments. This can be seen by changing the above evaluation argument a bit.

P1: I wore my mittens and my hands got cold after awhile.
P2: It was very cold today.

C: My prediction was partly right.

Now for the next prediction argument.

P1: I wear mittens and my hands stay warm in pretty cold weather.
P2: In very cold weather, mittens keep my hands warm for awhile.
P3: It is very cold today.

C: If I wear two pair of mittens, I might keep my hands warm.

The previous evaluation argument changed the first two prediction premises and lead to the third. The conclusion was a new prediction, a very small but important plan for the child. Of course a parent could have told her about colder weather and mittens, or that wearing more clothes does keep you warmer longer. But eventually, the child needs to come up with all the premises (evidence) and the conclusions. That is the critical step in becoming independent and adaptive. The next figure illustrates the inductive thinking process.

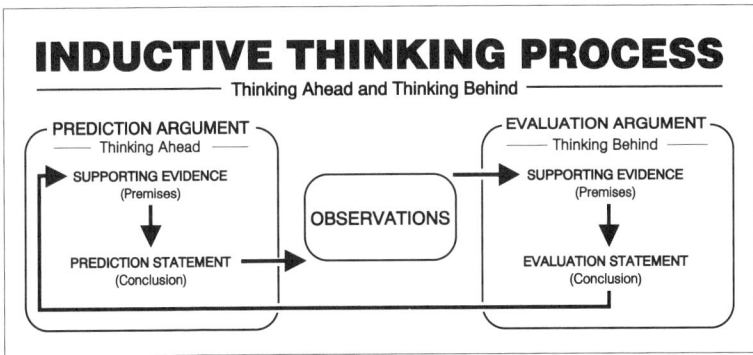

INDUCTIVE THINKING PROCESS
Thinking Ahead and Thinking Behind

PREDICTION ARGUMENT
Thinking Ahead

SUPPORTING EVIDENCE
(Premises)

PREDICTION STATEMENT
(Conclusion)

OBSERVATIONS

EVALUATION ARGUMENT
Thinking Behind

SUPPORTING EVIDENCE
(Premises)

EVALUATION STATEMENT
(Conclusion)

Inductive thinking helps control other behavior. Predictions act as conditions that set the occasion for part or all of the activity task and self-management behaviors. Evaluations act as consequences. They can reinforce or correct predictions and activity behaviors. By learning to behave inductively, children gain better control over their behavior. When they do so according to the Principles of Family, they behave ethically.

TEACHING THE INDUCTIVE PROCESS

Teaching inductive behavior begins as soon as your children can say simple sentences and undertake simple tasks like dressing or feeding themselves. As soon as you start to teach these tasks, you begin to teach inductive behavior.

The content of initial inductive behavior includes answers to: (1) Which task needs to be done? (2) What resources do I use? (3) When do I start and stop? (4) With whom do I work? (5) Where is the task performed? (6) What are the consequences? (7) How do I do the task? These questions form the heart of any activity contingency—its conditions, behaviors and consequences. Together they yield a plan. But to teach children to think inductively, you first focus on one of these pieces just before or during the activity. You bring their inductive behavior right next to or inside the activity.

Use statements and questions to model, prompt, test and provide consequences for inductive behavior. Initially, statements model inductive behavior. Later, statements and questions prompt the child to behave inductively. Finally, questions are used to test the child's inductive behavior. From this point it is a simple matter to expand the inductive behavior across a range of activities, and then refine it.

Initial Teaching

For adults, much of inductive behavior is private. Moreover, many activities that initially required inductive behavior become automatic. The contingencies have not changed, therefore further inductive behavior is not needed. But to teach children to think inductively, you will need to model the process with statements and questions.

Modeling. The modeling step demonstrates the inductive process and has two parts: the predictive and evaluation arguments. The first precedes behavior and the second follows it. The words used and the activity in which modeling takes place should be familiar to the child. The following example focuses on the materials needed for drawing.

For drawing pictures you will need paper and crayons. How do I know? I have drawn many pictures using them. [Child draws.]

Look at these drawings. See, I was right. You can draw with paper and crayons.

In the first part, the evidence follows the prediction. In the second, the evidence is presented first, with the evaluation statement second. The order is not crucial. The important thing is to present the two arguments as closely as possible to the task or self-management behavior to which they refer. In the above example, the evaluation argument could have been presented as the first drawing is being done. Here is another example.

> By scrubbing the dishes like this [demonstrates], and then rinsing them like this [demonstrates], you will get them clean. I know because it has worked every time I've done it. Give it a try. [Child imitates behavior.]
>
> See. You scrubbed and rinsed this dish like I said, and it is sparkling clean.

The inductive behavior focused on what task behaviors, scrubbing and rinsing, were needed to produce the consequence of clean dishes. The child does as predicted and the dishes become clean.

You can model inductive behavior with any activity you participate in or that you teach your child to do. Just look at the range of things you are going to teach and the list of activities that your child will participate in. It is very informal teaching, but it is powerful and important.

Prompting. After you have modeled some part of the activity contingency once or twice, you move to prompting. Statements and questions are used. Here is an example that parallels the above on drawing.

> So what do you need to draw pictures with today? (Child replies.) I agree because that is what you needed last time. (Child draws.)
>
> Was your prediction about needing the crayons and paper correct? (Child replies.) What told you so? (Child replies.)

This time the parent prompted the prediction and supplied the evidence for it. For the evaluation, the parent prompted it by presenting the prediction about needing crayons and paper, and then asked for the supporting evidence, which would have been something like the child pointing to the drawings. The dishwashing example could follow the same course.

> Besides scrubbing, what do you need to do to get the dishes clean? (Child replies.) How do you know? (Child replies.) Yes, that made them clean each time we did them. (Child washes.)

What was our prediction about how to get the dishes clean? (Child replies.) Was it correct? (Child replies). These dishes are really clean and so is your inductive thinking!

In both the prediction and evaluation, the parent is prompting the child by supplying part of the content. The parent follows the child's second reply with a statement that rewards the inductive behavior.

Testing. Questions form the foundation of testing. You simply ask for a prediction and its evidence, or the evaluation and its evidence. Of course, you reward your children when correct, and you may have to prompt or correct them if they are a little off, but initially, allow a lot of latitude. Refinement teaching will deal with getting at the critical evidence and the appropriate language. Here are the tests for the above behavior. "CR" stands for "child replies."

How do you get the dishes clean? (CR) How do you know? (CR) We will see.

Was your prediction correct about getting clean dishes? (CR) What told you so? (CR) Right once again. Clear thinking and clean dishes! [Big hug.]

Notice that the parent defined the term "prediction" in context. You teach most of the language of inductive behavior during expansion teaching; but if your child is a little older, you can start off with some of it.

Expansion Teaching

Use four expansions. The first expands your children's use of inductive behavior across a range of activities. The last three expand their understanding and use of the language of induction, contingencies and evidence. These three expansions make the behavior more effective within any activity. Shortly after you start the first expansion, the other three can begin. There is no need to separate them as long as you do the teaching across a number of activities and fairly often.

Teaching Inductive Behavior Across Familiar Activities. Once an activity has become routine, you just do the activity task. No thinking ahead or behind is needed. You are on automatic. But children have a long way to go to get to that point. Even if they can perform some of their activities without behaving inductively, it is important to have them do so.

You break this expansion into two parts. First, you keep teaching your children by modeling the inductive process for new activities, whether making paper dolls, drawing pictures, learning to skate, or building models. What you will notice is that you gradually move to tests much faster.

Second, you talk to your children about their predictions and evaluations outside the activities. At first you ask for their predictions just a little before and their evaluation just after. Then you gradually move to the night before or the day after. Eventually, you will find your children starting this talk. This is the final test, and indicates your success as a teacher and theirs as learners. They will start the conversation because their task success has reinforced them for interacting with you and behaving inductively. Here is an example of a parent-child reading activity.

> I look forward to our reading tonight. What will we need? (CR: A book and a place to sit.) How can we do it? (CR: I sit next to you and hold the book, and we take turns reading sentences.) And what will happen when we do it that way? (CR: We enjoy it and don't get tired of reading.) How do you know we will enjoy it? (CR: We have before.) You sure know a lot about our reading activity. [Hug.]

The start of this example focuses on asking about multiple contingency components: the resources, behaviors, and consequences of the activity. But the parent requests evidence for only one, the consequence. This interaction ends by reinforcing inductive behavior and the interaction with the parent as well.

A few interactions later, you need only ask a simple question like, "Have you thought about our reading activity for tonight?" Eventually, your child will begin the conversation with something like, "Dad, I found a book I would like us to read. Could we read it next?" From here the conversation takes whatever course seems appropriate. The father could ask, "Should we read like we usually do, or do you have another way?" When child-initiated inductive behavior begins outside the context of an activity, your children are thinking ahead and behind independently and adaptively.

A powerful prompt for this inductive behavior is having children participate in family activity planning. They may not contribute much at this early point, but they will see the model of the inductive process and family interaction. Once child-initiated inductive behavior begins, the natural reinforcers in the family system will keep it going. The next three expansion teaching procedures make it more powerful within any activity.

Teaching the Language of Inductive Behavior. You want to teach the more complex language of induction to your children because it facilitates communication—it focuses their questions and answers, as well as any statements made about their activities.

There are a number of words and phrases that apply to inductive behavior. At the most inclusive level, the terms *prediction, observation* and *evaluation* are the basic components. The prediction is always about partial or complete contingencies (conditions, behavior, consequences, and their relationships in an activity). A *hypothesis* is another word for prediction and a *confirmation* is another for evaluation—remembering that a confirmation can confirm or disprove a prediction. Each prediction and evaluation is made up of two parts: *supporting evidence statements* and a *prediction* or *evaluation statement.* Taken together, the supporting evidence statements and a prediction or evaluation statement form *arguments*—a *prediction argument* or an *evaluation argument.* Both of these arguments can range from *weak* to *strong.* If they are weak, the evidence does not give solid support for the prediction or evaluation. When looking at predictions and evaluations from the perspective of arguments, the pieces of supporting evidence are called *premises.* The prediction or evaluation statements are called *conclusions.* Premises lead to a conclusion. Ideally, the premises (evidence) strongly support (give credence to) the conclusion. You can remember this language by using the inductive thinking process figure.

Moving from the everyday to the technical language is easy. All you do is pair the everyday, familiar terms with the technical ones, or give your children a simple definition in the context of performing inductive behavior. Here are some examples.

What do you think, or predict, you will need for washing dishes?

Why do you think so, or what evidence do you have?

How do you know, or what is your supporting evidence?

How do you know, or what evidence supports your prediction?

What have you seen or observed that supports your prediction?

Was your prediction right or wrong? How would you evaluate it?

To tell me how your prediction was correct or incorrect is to evaluate it. How would you evaluate your prediction?

How do you know, or what supporting evidence do you have for your evaluation?

After a few pairings, you present only the language of inductive behavior.

What do you predict you will need for our activity?

What supporting evidence do you have for that prediction ?

What evidence did you observe to support your conclusion?

What is your evaluation of your prediction?

At this point, your children will understand the basics of the language. The language of arguments can wait for school, if desired. You can ask your children to make predictions about the stories you read together and to evaluate their predictions, asking for evidence. You only have to do it a few times during a story.

Once your children understand the language of induction, you can start to teach them to use it. You begin to model it in a few familiar activities, and then in the new ones they learn about. As you move to prompting and testing, their inductive behavior will begin to imitate yours. If it does not, the following correction will usually take care of the matter.

What do you predict we need for our reading activity? (CR: A book and a place to sit.) Can you say it like I do, "I predict we will need a book and a place to sit?" Give it a try. (CR: I predict we will need a book and a place to sit.) That's it.

A few corrections like this and the child will begin to respond with complete sentences across the range of language. You can help this process by asking for complete sentences even before the language of inductive behavior is taught.

Teaching the Language of Contingencies. Inductive behavior predicts, observes and evaluates the contingencies of an activity. Thus, it is helpful to teach your children to see and talk about activities as contingencies. The reasons for doing so are the same as those for teaching inductive behavior. The process is also the same. You teach your children to understand and use four terms: condition, behavior, consequence and contingency when making predictions and evaluations of their activities. The term resources can also be taught as another word for conditions. Here is how the pairing could be done.

What is needed, or what conditions help us read at night?

How do you do that, or what behavior is needed?

What happens, or what is the consequence of doing that?

Once the child's use of these terms has been refined, "contingency" can be taught. Here is one way to do it.

When you can predict the resources, behaviors, and consequences of an activity, you know the contingency of the activity. What is the contingency for doing the dishes? Can you give me the resources first? (CR: The resources are dirty dishes, soap, water, and dish towel.) What are the behaviors of the dishwashing contingency? (CR: The behaviors are scraping, scrubbing, rinsing, wiping, and putting away). What are the consequences of the dishwashing contingency? (CR: The consequences are clean dishes, and a good feeling that the job is done.) So what contingency did you just tell me about? (CR: The dishwashing contingency.) You understood "contingency" the first time!

Next time, and across many activities, the child gradually describes the contingency with no prompting. Eventually, you ask: "What do you predict the contingency will be for our reading activity?" This talk is a little strange, but it is accurate. The talk of the architect, surgeon, lawyer, or any other technical person seems strange to those who have not been taught to use it; but each is useful because it allows them to handle their respective activities.

Teaching planning is teaching a child to behave inductively towards activity contingencies.

Looking for Evidence. Looking for evidence primarily relates to prediction arguments. In the previous examples the evidence was of one kind—enumeration of instances of the activity. What was done in the past worked, so it should work again. But we often use two additional kinds of evidence. The second type is analogous evidence, that is, something is like something else.

P1:	I cooked broccoli for six minutes in the microwave.
P2:	Cauliflower is similar to broccoli.

C:	So I would cook cauliflower for about six minutes, too.

The conclusion is supported by an analogous relationship. The evidence to support the prediction of wearing two pairs of mittens could have come from analogy.

P1:	When it is very cold, my mittens do not keep my hands warm.
P2:	When I wear more shirts, I keep warmer.
P3:	Shirts are like mittens.

C:	If I wear more mittens, I will keep warmer.

Both mittens and shirts are insulating. An analogy is presented, but the relationship has not been expressed. As a parent teaching your child, you can prompt the child to fill out the relationship.

The third form of evidence is statistical—something does not always lead to something else, but it does so at least some of the time. The words "usually," "often" and "most of the time" indicate statistical evidence is being given. The evidence for the last two arguments could have been partially statistical.

P1:	Broccoli is a vegetable.
P2:	Most of the vegetables take about six minutes to cook in the microwave.

C:	Broccoli will cook in about six minutes.

P1:	Mittens are clothing.
P2:	Often when I wear more clothing, I keep warmer.

C:	If I wear more mittens, I will keep my hands warmer.

Often the conclusions of arguments with such evidence contain words or phrases like "about," "may help" or "a good chance." They indicate that close observation will be required for the evaluation argument.

Knowing about the types of evidence helps you model and prompt looking for it, and makes it easier to teach. You present evidence across the types as you model inductive behavior across activities. You use these forms of evidence every day of your life. By being aware of them, you can model them more clearly. The prompts for this "looking for evidence" expansion are also facilitated by this knowledge.

1. What has been done before? (Enumeration prompt.)
   What has been needed before?
   What has happened before?

2. What usually would work here? (Statistical prompt.)
   What is usually needed here?
   What may happen?

3. What is this like? (Analogy prompt.)
   What do we need in a similar activity?
   What would happen in other activities like this one?

The variations in prompts occur because the inductive behavior may be about any part of an activity contingency. These are only some of the possibilities, but they take you a long way toward teaching inductive behavior based on strong evidence.

The problem of evidence and the support it gives to a conclusion has been a persistent concern in philosophy and science. But your children are not there yet. Your future philosophers and scientists need some everyday practice with the inductive process.

Refinement Teaching

Refinement teaching begins at about the same time as expansion teaching. The consequences of initial and expansion teaching are keeping the behavior going. Now it needs some polish. First, you want inductive behavior to begin before or at the start of an activity (a short latency). Second, you want accurate prediction, evaluation and evidence statements.

Quick-starting inductive behavior will usually result from the reinforcing consequences that accompany your initial and expansion teaching. You can also directly reinforce it. Consider the following examples:

You're getting quick at telling me what is needed and how to do it.

Boy, that was a fast answer. You really know about this activity.

If your child does not begin to state or ask you about what conditions, behaviors or consequences are related to an activity, you can prompt by saying something like this:

When activities are hard or new, you should always try to think about what is needed and how to do it before you start. You can also ask me if you are not sure.

Now all you do is reinforce such behavior. The following statement follows the parent's answer to a child's question about an activity:

I am glad you asked. It tells me you are thinking ahead, or inductively, about what you are going to do. [Hug.]

The statement and hug are designed to reinforce fast inductive behavior, as well as linking the phrases "thinking ahead" and "thinking inductively."

Refining the accuracy of predictions, evaluations, and evidence is relative to what you have taught. Here are four statements that reinforce accuracy.

That is complete and accurate evidence.

That's the same prediction I would have made.

Your prediction is correct and shows me you are thinking about this activity.

I think you know this activity better than I do. Accurate thinking.

Eventually, the inclusive reinforcing statements like, "That's very accurate inductive behavior" will be enough. At the point when they can begin to behave inductively across a range of activities and use at least some of the language of inductive behavior, your children are ready to learn the self-management strategies. Remember, however, that refinement teaching continues, because children are continually moving on to new activities with more complex contingencies. Thus, inductive behavior needs continuing refinement, since it uses evidence that is accumulated over a lifetime.

TEACHING THE OLDER AND THE SECOND CHILD

The above teaching focused on the younger child. It will usually take a number of months before your child learns to behave inductively, and longer to use the language of induction to talk about activities. If you begin such teaching with a child of five, six or seven, you would most likely move a little faster through initial and expansion teaching.

For the child of eight to twelve, start with teaching planning, because a plan is inductive behavior. Include the child in family activity planning as much as possible, using the language of inductive behavior. Teach the child to think inductively in this context, and encourage him or her to do it outside of the planning activity as well. It is especially important to point out the positive consequences that result from activities that were planned.

Once you have taught one or more of your children to behave inductively, they can help you teach it to younger siblings. All you need to do is demonstrate what you did with them, and then occasionally observe to prompt and reinforce the inductive teaching; but do not rely entirely on this. Use it to expand and refine your own teaching.

SUMMARY

Thinking ahead builds a prediction. When you behave, you observe the changes that were important to the prediction. Thinking behind builds an evaluation of the prediction based on the evidence observed. The evaluation is used in making future predictions. This cycling process is called inductive thinking. All of us use it. To teach it to your children, initially teach the process during familiar activities, using models, prompts, tests, and consequences all along the way. Once your children have the basics of inductive thinking, expand the process across activities, first within those that they know and then to new ones. As their inductive thinking skills improve, you continue expansion teaching by introducing the language of induction. Use the figure on page 45 as a prompt for the inductive process and for the language of induction. Next, teach the language of contingencies, which includes talking about the conditions, behaviors and consequences of an activity. For the final expansion, you teach them to look for and work from a range of evidence. Shortly after you begin expansion teaching, you start to refine the speed, accuracy and consistency of inductive thinking. When their inductive thinking becomes strong across activities, you can begin to teach them the self-management strategies. At this point, their inductive thinking becomes part of their self-management behavior.

CHAPTER 6

ORGANIZING

Organizing is the strategy of efficiency. It saves time and effort. The child, the adult and the corporate group use the same process of organizing. All identify, locate, transfer and arrange resources to perform activities. The strategy of organizing clarifies thinking and economizes actions. Families benefit in several ways. Your own activities take less time, and by teaching the strategy to your children, you expend less time and energy organizing for them. You will have more time for what you want and need to do, and your children will be more independent and responsible.

ORGANIZING STRATEGY

The figure on page 61 illustrates the steps and questions, called elements, of the organizing strategy. The first step is to identify the resources needed to begin and complete the activity. The resources needed at this point (1a) include people, materials and tools. It is also important to know how much or how many of each is needed (1b). If you identify both the type and the amount of resources correctly, you take the first step toward avoiding delays and conserving resources as the activity progresses.

Organizing continues with locating the resources (2). If the locations of the resources do not spring to mind or are not specified in the activity plan, the first thing you ask is how they can be located (2a). Two kinds of knowledge give you help: knowing the classes (categories) into which the resources fall and the sources that identify where such resources are located. Grocery stores sell all kinds of food. Hardware stores sell anything to do with the home or shop. There is some overlap. The Yellow Pages is a good example of a source for locating a classification. Once you have a couple of ways to locate the resources, you must find where they are (2b). With the phone book and a telephone, you can locate a great deal.

Transferring the located resources (3) may take several substeps. First, you have to identify where the resources are needed (3a). The activity may take place in one or more locations, with the latter requiring a distribution of resources. The resources of an activity, especially a complex one like building a home, may be needed at different times. To have them at an earlier time complicates the task; having them too late slows down the task. Thus, it is important to identify when they need to be transferred to the activity location (3b). How they are transferred (3c) depends on the identification of applicable and available modes of transportation.

The final step of organizing arranges the resources for use (4). The first element asks how they can be arranged in the activity location (4a). The child arranges paper and crayons on the floor or table so the drawing activity can be performed smoothly, without undo interruption. In building and manufacturing, answering the how of arrangement often requires elaborate planning for the same reasons of smooth, uninterrupted work flow.

Arranging transferred resources takes time. Identifying when they must be arranged (4b) is a continuation of transferring them to the activity location. For the child drawing a picture on the floor, the question is answered by, "As soon as they are transferred, because they are needed there from the start of drawing." But in building and manufacturing, the arrangement may be ongoing; a little bit at a time is arranged in the work area. Even with the correct arrangement of resources, organizing is not complete. The final step is to return reusable or unused resources to their location, so that the next time they are needed they can be quickly located (4c). The child puts away the crayons, paper and drawings. The jacket is hung up and the dirty clothes deposited in the hamper. For children, this element of organizing is often called picking up after themselves. One gets the environment ready for another activity or for others who are going to use it.

If you get stuck answering the organizing process questions during a task, your activity plan is incomplete. You need to return to planning. If during planning you get stuck answering them, you need the learning strategy to solve an organizing problem. Usually organizing will flow smoothly unless you do not have knowledge of the activity task behaviors.

ORGANIZING STRATEGY

1. **IDENTIFY THE RESOURCES**
   a. What resources are needed? (people, materials, tools)
   b. How much of each is needed?

2. **LOCATE THE RESOURCES**
   a. How can they be located? (classification and sources)
   b. Where are they located?

3. **TRANSFER THE RESOURCES**
   a. Where are they needed?
   b. When are they needed?
   c. How can they be transferred?

4. **ARRANGE THE RESOURCES**
   a. How can they be arranged?
   b. When should the arrangement be completed?
   c. What needs to be returned when the task is completed?

The rest of this chapter focuses on teaching your children the strategy of organizing. Because you, the adult, can use the organizing strategy as illustrated, you can begin to teach yourself to use the strategy through planning an activity as outlined in Chapter 10. For your children, learning requires that teaching take a careful step-by-step approach. Because organizing is the first strategy you teach them, this careful approach is especially important.

TEACHING ORGANIZING

Organizing occurs in all children's activities. To begin with, they organize in activities like playing (drawing, dolls, blocks), dressing, eating, toileting, helping you with around-the-house tasks, and reading with you. You initially teach organizing during these familiar activities. They learn to recognize the need for organizing, its language, and its steps. You teach six terms: identify, resources, locate, transfer, arrange, and return. If your children already know some of these, the teaching will proceed faster. The teaching can begin a little after your children begin to speak in sentences of a few words.

Initial Teaching

Modeling. Begin the initial teaching of organizing with months of modeling. You have to organize for your child, so why not model, using the language of organizing that tells what you are doing. The child gets concise examples of the language and sees the process of organizing across a range of activities. It is a healthy interaction; and the more the child participates, the more fun it becomes. Talk in simple sentences, defining what you are saying as you go. Let your children participate when they can. Here is an example. What you do is in brackets.

> Let's organize for making and eating breakfast. First some resources. We need a bowl, cereal, milk, honey, a spoon and napkin. They are located in the cupboard. Let's transfer them to the table. [Get resources.] Here is the bowl, cereal, milk, honey, spoon and napkin. [Point out resources as you arrange them.] Now, I arrange them on the table so we can make breakfast. [Make breakfast.] Let's eat. [Feed child.] Breakfast is all eaten. Let's finish organizing by putting all these resources away and cleaning up. [Point to resource, put away, and clean up.]

During initial teaching, you focus on the four steps of organizing and the returning element. You do not talk about or consider the other elements of organizing at this time. That is part of expansion teaching. During this modeling, you are teaching other things like the naming of objects. For the older child with more language skills, your talk is just more sophisticated. Here is an example.

Let me show you how to organize for breakfast. The first part is to identify what resources you need. We need (etc.).... The second part of organizing is locating the resources. The bowls are in the.... The third part of organizing is transferring the resources to where they are needed. Can you help me by transferring the cereal and milk? [Transfer the resources.] The fourth part of organizing is arranging the resources. Here is how we arrange them for breakfast. [Demonstrate.] And now we eat. [Eat.] We finish organizing by putting the resources away. You put the bowls and spoons in the sink, and I will put the rest away. [Talk through the process as you demonstrate putting away and cleaning up.]

During this model you can ask older children what some of the resources are, where they are located, and how they are arranged. The basic rule is to involve them as much as possible in whatever activity you are modeling.

Prompting. After young children can name a number of objects in the activities and say a few telegraphic sentences like, "I want a banana," begin to prompt predictions of organizing by using questions about the language of organizing. Also, have them repeat the step names if they do not say them when asked. This simple correction is usually all you need. The child's responses are in parentheses.

It is time for breakfast. So what do we do? (CR: Organize.) The first step is to identify the resources. What is the first step of organizing? (CR: Identify the resources.). Can you tell me what they are? (CR) That is most of them. The only resource left is the honey. The second step of organizing is to locate the resources. What is the second step? (CR: Locate the resources.) Where are the resources located? (CR) Now let's do the third step of organizing, transfer the resources. What is the third step? (CR: Transfer the resources.) And the last step is to arrange the resources. What is the last step? (CR: Arrange the resources.) Let's transfer and arrange. [Transfer and arrange.] Can you help me make the breakfast? (CR: Yes.) [Make and eat breakfast.] That was a good breakfast. Let's finish arranging the resources by returning them. What is the last part of organizing? (CR: Return the resources.) Let's do it together. [Return.] It's more fun for me when you help with organizing and making breakfast.

In two or three interactions, begin to ask the child the steps without the prompt of first naming it. There may be a step the child forgets. Prompt by giving the answer and asking the child to repeat it. Gradually, the child will name all the steps as you ask for them and be able to perform all the organizing. You are fading the prompts at this point. How long it takes to fade the prompts depends on the language skills of the child. When you fade prompts, you are moving toward testing.

Testing. You model in many activities, you prompt in two or three, and you test in the ones you prompted. When you have totally faded the prompts, you are testing. You want the child to identify that it is time to organize, to use the language of organizing, and to do as much of the organizing as he or she is physically capable of doing. Here is what the test and the response would look like.

What is it time for? (CR: Breakfast.) What is it we have to do? (CR: Organize.) If I help, can you organize us for breakfast using all the words of organizing? (CR: Yes.) So, what do we do? (CR)

At this point the child walks you through organizing, just like you did in the model. If the child gets stuck or forgets, give the step or name the resources. Eventually, there will be no mistakes in the activities you are focusing on for testing. Only when there are no errors has the test been passed. Moving from modeling to prompting to testing is a gradual and continual process. You may have to prompt for some period of time; but one day you will find that the child seems to know how to organize for the activity, and can use all the language.

Consequences. The consequences you provide or indicate through your statements, questions and actions point in two directions. First, they indicate that the child organized correctly. Second, they identify the natural consequences of organizing for the child or others.

You identified the resources and located them. You're getting the steps of organizing. Your organizing helps us get done quicker. Thanks. [Hug.]

What part of organizing did you do? (CR) Yes, you identified the resources and located them. Did it help us? (CR: Yes.) How? (CR: We got done quicker.) That's a good reason to organize together. [Handshake.]

Was your prediction about organizing for breakfast correct? (CR: Yes.) What is your evidence? (CR: We made breakfast and ate it.) Accurate prediction and evidence.

Also, quick little statements like "You remembered the hard step; I like that" are important to the ongoing stream of organizing during an activity.

Expansion Teaching

Four expansions are used: teaching the strategy across a range of familiar activities, the What Management Game, teaching the strategy elements, and using the strategy during family activity planning.

Teaching the Strategy Across Familiar Activities. For many familiar activities, you have already modeled both talking about and performing organizing. Thus, the major teaching tools are the prompt, test, and consequence.

[Prompt.] You have organizing down pat for breakfast. Can you do the same for our reading activity? (CR: Yes.) I think so too. Show me. (CR)

[Consequence.] You organized for reading without missing a step. When you help with the organizing, we have more time for reading.

Such an expansion works well for activities you participate in with your child or have time to watch. But there are those situations in which that is not the case, and you want to give a test that has little or no prompting associated with it.

[Test.] What are you going to do next? (CR: Draw.) Can you tell me how you will organize for drawing? (CR) That sounds like a workable plan to me. [Consequence.]

[Consequence—after activity.] You organized for drawing just like you planned. Great predicting. It sure helps me clean up the living room when you return your drawing materials. Thank you. [Hugs and kisses.]

This expansion can be used even if you participate in the activity. The advantage of this expansion is that it demands more thinking-ahead behavior. There is more planning to it, as the parent identifies. Of course, the child may forget part of the organizing. The prompt could be given like this:

[After activity.] It looks like you identified, located, transferred and arranged just about as you planned. What is the one thing you forgot? Look. (CR: I didn't return the crayons to my toy box.) Yes. If you do it, you help me keep the living room clean and neat. Can you do it? (CR: Yes.) Thank you.

If you modeled picking up the living room at about the same time you asked about returning the toys, two things could happen: the child may begin to help you, and on other occasions he may just start to pick up the living room when he puts his toys or drawing materials away.

What Management Game. This expansion widens the range of activities that the child sees as needing organizing. When you are in the store, traveling, or watching television, have the child first identify what step you point out.

[At the store where a clerk is arranging a product on a shelf.] What step of organizing is that person performing? (CR: Arranging.) I think so, too. Remember when you see a step of organizing to ask me if I can name it. [At check-out counter.] What step of organizing is the checkout person doing? (CR: Transferring the food from one place to another.) Another statement I agree with. Do you want to get evidence by asking him? (CR)

If you think the child is wrong, correct by saying something like, "I think it is transferring, because it moves the resources from one place to another." If you really want the child to gather evidence, this is a great place for asking the person doing the organizing. Because others may not have the language of organizing, you may want to model how to ask for evidence the first few times. That model names one or two steps of organizing to give the person the context of your question; e.g., "Pardon me, my son and I were wondering if you would call placing the items on the shelf transferring or arranging?"

After you have asked about the organizing steps three or four times, you can begin the game by asking, "Is that organizing or not organizing?" or "Do you think that person is organizing or not?" If it is organizing, you would continue to ask about the steps as done above or simply ask, "How do you know it is organizing?" The answer will usually be the naming of a strategy step.

Teaching Strategy Elements. This expansion increases the probability that the organizing strategy will be successful within any activity. Adding the elements requires that the child have beginning reading skills and is best done during your teaching activity first mentioned in Chapter 3. The reading skills allow the organizing strategy, presented as a poster in the appendix, to be used to model and prompt the strategy elements.

For young children, it may be necessary to "pre-teach" reading the words: organizing, resource, identify, locate, transfer, arrange, return and complete. Because your children can use these words fluently by this time, they will learn them quickly. Present the words with flash cards. Say something like, "You know these words. They are about organizing." Model reading each word, have them say it with you, and then by themselves. After you have done three words, repeat the first one. After they have three words, add another; and when that is learned, add another. Repeat until all words are said without delay. Remember to shuffle the cards so reading and not order controls success. You do not have to teach all the words in one sitting. If you taught your children to read with a phonics program, sound out the words.

Modeling and Prompting. Because of the child's skill at organizing across an array of activities by this time, begin the element expansion with models and prompts used back-to-back for each organizing step.

Organizing for some activities requires that we ask a number of questions for each strategy step. This poster of the organizing strategy gives those questions. [Point to poster.] Can you read the first step of organizing as I point? [Point. Child reads step and elements.] For breakfast [Point to 1a], what are the resources needed? (CR) [Point to 1b] How much of each resource do you need? (CR) [Prompt child for each resource.] So, you know what resources and how much of each is needed. When you plan an activity for the first time, you need to follow these questions so that you don't forget.

You have introduced and connected organizing to planning and shown the child that she already knows the answers for one or more activities. The lesson continues with step two.

[Point to step 2.] Now read the second step and its questions. (CR) [Point to 2a.] You know where the resources are located for breakfast. If you did not, how would you find out? (CR: I would ask you.) That's right. You could also look in other places. Where would you look? (CR: In the dishwasher.) [Point to 2a.] See, you know two ways to locate resources. [Point to 2b.] When you ask or look, you find out where the resources are located.

[Point to step 3.] Can you read the third step? (CR) [Point to 3a.] For each activity, resources are needed somewhere. Where are they needed for breakfast? (CR: At the table.) [Point to 3b.] When are the breakfast resources needed? (CR: Before we eat.) [Point to 3c.] Since you know when, how can the resources be transferred? (CR: We carry them to the table.) So you can do all of step three for breakfast.

[Point to step 4.] Can you read step 4? (CR) [Point to 4a.] How can the resources be arranged for breakfast? (CR) That is how we do it each morning. [Point to 4b.] Can you read 4b and answer it? (CR: Before we sit down to eat.) [Point to 4c.] What about 4c? (CR: Everything on the table.) That's right. See, you can already do all these steps and questions for breakfast. Would you like to plan a new way to organize for breakfast tomorrow? (CR: Yes.)

By reading and answering the questions with your prompt, the child has acted as his or her own model. You may have to help with an answer or two because you're talking about organizing a little differently, but usually that is about all you need to do. Doing this format two times is enough. On the next occasion, use another activity the child participates in daily. During such teaching, the parent is fulfilling the responsibility side of the family principles of health, representation, membership, quality and adaptation.

Prompting and Testing. As you prompt and test—it is a matter of degree once again—you use the organizing strategy as a planning guide. You plan different ways to organize. The extent to which you help the child is dependent on the extent to which you move away from activities organized by the child.

[Point to organizing strategy.] When we plan with the organizing strategy, we try to find answers for each question. Should we plan an organization for breakfast? (CR: Yes.) Okay, read 1a and answer it if you can. (CR: We eat cereal and drink juice, so we need ....) Could you use cups instead of glasses or the bigger bowls? (CR: Yes.) So, there are different resources you could use and still make and eat breakfast. Read 1b and answer. (CR) So, how many do not change? Can you read 2a? (CR) [Points.] Could you answer 2a? (CR: I could ask you or look around if I did not find them.) Is there another way to locate them? (CR: I don't know.) If we don't have any cereal or honey, where do we get them? (CR: At the store.) So the store is another place to locate them. Read 2b. (CR) You have been to the store with me. Do you know where the cereal and honey are located? (CR: Yes.) Read 3a. (CR) As you know, we sit and eat at the kitchen table. Is there anywhere else we could eat? (CR: At the dining room table.) Do you want to eat there? (CR: No. I like the kitchen.) Okay. Read 3b. (CR) Could we change when we need the resources? (CR: No.) We could change the time a little for Saturday and Sunday, but not much. Read 3c. (CR) Could we change how we transfer the resources? (CR: No.) Just you and I could carry them. Read 4a. (CR) Could we change how the resources are arranged? (CR: Yes. I could sit where you do and you could sit over there.) So we could at least sit differently. Does that mean we would have to place the resources on the table differently? (CR: Not much.) Read 4b. (CR) Could you change when the resources are arranged? (CR: No. They still have to be there when we start to eat.) Good. Read 4c. (CR) Could we change what we return? (CR: No.) You are right. If we did, the table would not be cleaned off. So are there a lot of changes you want to make or could make in organizing for breakfast? (CR: No.) Do you want to change sitting places for a while? (CR: Yes.)

The organizing strategy has been placed in the context of planning. Moreover, inductive thinking has been emphasized throughout.

Family Activity Planning. Family activity planning, described at length in Chapter 10, provides a real test for your strategy element teaching. Start by asking your children to plan a new organization for one of their activities. Provide the poster and follow along. Prompt only if there are some obvious things the child did not think of. This is the first phase of planning (designing a plan). You can do the second phase after you implement any changes. At this point, simply ask, "Did you like the way you organized? Did the new plan work?" The answers will lead to accepting the plan or to replanning. From this point your child can contribute more to the organizational side of any family plan.

Refinement Teaching

Refinement teaching begins during activities in which the child organizes on a regular basis. To increase the accuracy, consistency and speed of organizing, prompts and consequences are the primary vehicles.

[Prompt.] If we get organized real fast, we will have time to stop and look at the animals in the pet store. How fast can you get dressed?

[Consequence—after organizing behavior of getting dressed for shopping.] That was fast! We have lots of time for the animals. [Big hug.]

There is an access consequence waiting if there is time for it. Fast organizing creates the time to look at the animals in the local pet store. Tests are simply non-prompted situations that provide the opportunity for speedy organizing. A consequence statement may follow.

You are a fast organizer. You got dressed and ready for school and got breakfast all organized before I finished getting dressed for work. That is amazingly fast organizing. Thanks. [Hugs and kisses.]

Additionally, you want to reinforce organizing in places in which it has not been taught, and point out the relationship of the organizing consequences to the Principles of Family.

Thank you for getting the table set for dinner. Getting things organized for me makes getting dinner ready easier. You have been doing that almost every day, and I appreciate it. [Hug.] It is a good example of following the principle of membership. [Point to the Principles of Family poster.]

Returning your toys carefully to your toy box shows me you are an excellent organizer and are trying to follow the family principle of conservation. I like both the organizing and the following.

A statement like this every day or two over the course of years helps to define what each Principle of Family represents.

You may need to correct organizing occasionally during refinement. The main tool is the use of natural consequences. If your children are not dressed to go somewhere, they go as they are. If it is time to read to them and their toys are not put away, they miss reading or some part of it. Of course, there are extenuating circumstances now and then, like when they make a good effort but fail to be ready or cleaned up on time. Allow the time needed, prompt if needed during the activity, and provide consequences to show that you really value organizing and how useful it is in saving time. If you do these things, your children will become well organized.

CHAPTER 7

HELPING

Helping enables people to get along with one another and complete their tasks, and leads to informal teaching and learning. Our language has a family of words that relate to helping. *Aiding* suggests that the helper takes a necessary role in the task. *Assisting* denotes a subordinate role by the helper, one that makes the task easier or more fun. *Supporting* is indirect helping that ranges from providing essential resources to not interfering with another's task. All forms of helping can be viewed as working cooperatively with others to enable them to complete their tasks. In following the family principle of membership, we regularly help one another.

HELPING AS A PAIR OF STRATEGIES

Let's look at helping from the perspective of both the helper and the helpee (the one being helped). The figure on the following page presents steps for each. First, the helper or helpee identifies the need to help (step 1). If the offer to or the request for help (2) is accepted (3), helping proceeds and ends in thanks by the helpee (5). If thanked, the helper accepts the thanks (5). If the offer to or the request for help is rejected (4), helping does not occur and the rejection is accepted. Thus, there are four forms of helping: the helper's offer can be accepted or rejected, as can the helpee's asking.

There are a couple of minor variations in the strategies. First, one starts to help as soon as the need is identified when it can reduce a

73

potential danger or prevent an accident. Second, there is often an extra step in accepting the offer or the request: the helper accepts the helpee's thanks by saying something like, "You're welcome," or giving a nod and a smile.

HELPING STRATEGIES

—— HELPER'S STRATEGY ——

1. IDENTIFY THE NEED TO HELP
2. OFFER TO HELP
3. IF OFFER ACCEPTED,
   HELP AS NEEDED
4. IF OFFER REJECTED,
   ACCEPT REJECTION
5. IF THANKED FOR HELPING,
   ACCEPT THANKS

—— HELPEE'S STRATEGY ——

1. IDENTIFY THE NEED FOR HELP
2. ASK FOR HELP
3. IF REQUEST ACCEPTED,
   PROCEED WITH TASK
4. IF REQUEST REJECTED,
   ACCEPT REJECTION
5. THANK HELPER WHEN DONE

TEACHING HELPING

Initial Teaching

Initial teaching begins by teaching the acceptance forms of helping. Once these are taught, introduce the rejection forms. For all forms of helping, you model, prompt, test and provide consequences.

Modeling. With very young children, you already help them do almost everything. Use these opportunities for the early modeling of helping. Even if your child can't speak, the model is useful.

I see you need a little help getting the food in your mouth. Let me help you. Is that okay? Well, I know you would say yes if you could. So here, let me assist in guiding the spoon to your mouth. See how easy it is with a little help? You're doing just fine, and I know you would thank me if you could. How about some more help with that wonderful apricot-banana sauce you are eating? I know it is hard to hold that spoon, but you'll get it pretty soon.

This talk helps you as much as the child; you are rehearsing the steps of helping. With minor modification, you can change to modeling "asking for help."

(Child is crying.) I am glad you asked for help. If you could speak, you would say, "Could I have some help wiping my bottom?" Naturally, being your father, I would say, "Yes." Then I would make your bottom all clean and dry. Watch how I do it so you can learn. [Cleans and dries.] See? All clean and dry. What do you say? Thanks would be fine.

As soon as the child begins to speak simple sentences, interactive modeling can begin. Start with offering to help. This can be done in the family teaching activity or during activities like reading or playing with the child. Handing blocks to a child stacking them is a good opportunity.

Here is one way you help. First, you offer help. You could say, "Can I help you stack the blocks?" Say that. (CR) I would say, "Yes." Now help me by handing me the blocks to stack. (CR) When we are done, I thank you for helping. I say, "Thank you for helping." You say, "You're welcome" in return. Say that. (CR) That is one way to help.

Asking for help would be modeled in the same way.

Here is another way of helping. This time you ask for help. You start by saying something like, "Can you help me to stack the blocks?" Say that. (CR) I would say, "Yes." Then I would begin to help. [Helps.]

When we are done, you thank me for helping like before. What would you say? (CR) And I would say, "You're welcome." That is how helping is done when you ask. Do you think you can do it when you need help? (CR)

Modeling for two or three days is usually sufficient. Mealtime also provides a good opportunity to teach both asking for and offering to help. Asking to have something passed or offering to pass something occurs several times at each meal.

Prompting. Use the same setting to prompt helping. The "stacking of blocks" activity could be used again. Here is how the prompting might look.

I am going to stack blocks again. Could you help me? (CR: Yes.) How would you do it? (CR: Offer to help. I would say, "Can I help you?") Good. What would happen next? (CR: You would say, "Yes," and I would begin to help.) Okay, let's start. (CR: *Helps.*) Now that we are done stacking blocks, what happens? (CR: You thank me for helping.) Thank you. (CR: I say, "You're welcome," and we are all done.) You're getting the idea of how to offer help. [Hug.]

Here is the asking-for-help version.

Let's do asking for help. You're going to stack blocks and want some help. What do you do first? (CR: Ask, "Can you help me to stack the blocks?") And I say, "Yes." What next? (CR: You hand me blocks as I stack.) Let's do it. [Helps.] (CR: We are all done. Thank you.) You're welcome. I enjoyed helping. Do you think you can ask for it when you need help? (CR)

The number of times you need to prompt will depend on the language skills of your children and the extent to which they have seen helping modeled, not only by you, as done above, but by the full interactive model between both parents and other children.

Testing. The time will come when the prompts are no longer needed. You are testing. This is how it would look.

Can you do all the parts of offering me help? (CR: Yes.) Go to it. (CR: First, I say, "Do you need help?" Then you say, "Yes." I give you help like this. [*Helps.*] When we are done, you say, "Thank you.") Thank you for your help. (CR: And I say, "You're welcome.") That's it! You know all the steps of offering help. Can you offer help whenever you see the need for it? (CR: Yes.) [Kisses.]

The asking-for-help test would be the same. When the child has passed the test twice for either one of the helping forms, move to expansion teaching.

Consequences. During modeling, prompting and testing, you change the form of the consequences as you did during the teaching of organizing. The consequences for modeling focus on clear, fast responses.

You said that clearly, so we can keep going.

You are really listening; you got the answer the first time.

Very clear.

During prompting, your consequences focus on what was remembered and some of the acceptable variations of helping. You insert them as you move through the helping interaction.

You got it. That was the step you forgot before.

That is a nice way to thank me.

Each day you are remembering more about asking for help.

The consequences for testing occur at the end of the child's rendition of helping. This is the place for the more complete statement:

You got every step of the helping strategy right. Great work; and it only took four days to learn it! Fast learning. Let me give you a big hug.

The parent described the behavior, indicated consequences, and pointed to the rapid evolution of the behavior. Of course, the child could give the parent a big hug for good teaching.

The above examples focus on teaching the acceptance forms of helping. The rejection forms remain to be taught. You initially teach them in much the same way. Begin their teaching when your child begins to help and to see when to help without prompts. The initial teaching model might go like this:

[During helping.] You have just asked if you could help. So far, I have always said, "Yes." But there are times when the other person does not want help. Let's say I do not want help. I would say, "Thank you for offering, but I would like to do this by myself." Can you say that? (CR) If your help is not wanted, you say something simple like, "Okay." This shows you accept that the person did not want help.

Following this model, occasionally reject the child's offer to help. After the child demonstrates the acceptance of rejections, show the child how to reject help herself. Do the above, but put it in the context of the child not wanting help. You can prompt the child during activities to reject help by saying something like, "Do you want help, or would you like to try it by yourself?" If the child says, "By myself," prompt by asking, "How would you say the whole thing when you do not want help?" Given your models and earlier imitations, there should be no problem. After modeling, prompting and testing the child on the rejection format, begin expansion teaching.

Expansion Teaching

Expansion teaching begins when the initial teaching tests have been passed for each strategy. Begin expanding the rejection forms only after the child has mastered the acceptance forms across a range of activities.

Teaching the Strategy Across Familiar Activities. First, prompt helping in a range of activities in which the child participates. You can prompt at any point during an activity when helping could occur.

[Prompt.] What could you offer me here? (CR: Helping. Oh! Do you want some help with the dishes?)

The interaction would continue. You can prompt in the same way when siblings or peers are interacting. You can finish the interaction with a simple consequence statement.

[Consequence.] Once you knew, you did a nice job of offering and helping. Thank you.

If the child missed a step of helping, correct by telling her the step. Eventually, your prompting would not be needed, and only consequences would be used.

> [Consequence.] You spotted my need for help. I was not much in the mood for doing the dishes. Your help made doing them more enjoyable. Did you enjoy helping?

What Management Game. The second expansion across activities is the What Management Game. It insures that children will see the range of opportunities for helping outside of their immediate family. Since you have done the game with organizing, you do not need to model.

> Look at that man. Do you think he needs help? (CR: Yes.) How would you help him? (CR: Carry some of his bags.) That's the help I would give. If you spot where help is needed or is being given, will you point it out to me? (CR: Yes.)

This example prompts inductive thinking. You are asking for a prediction about helping, and you evaluate it. Additionally, you ask for the child to initiate it in the future. From this point, the child can be reinforced for identifying helping situations pointed out by either of you, and predicting how to help. It is important for you to include situations that are not helping, just to insure that the child does not simply answer "yes" automatically. The main consequence is access to an interaction that probes the child's knowledge of helping. At this point, you are beginning to refine helping.

With organizing, you asked about the strategy steps being performed by others. With helping, you ask how help could be done. The interaction can be changed slightly to stress asking for help.

> If you were that person, what would you ask for? (CR: Help.) How would you ask? (CR: Could you please help me move this table over there?) That is one of the ways I would ask for help, too.

The "How would you ask?" portion gets at the manner of asking, which will often indicate how the helping will be performed.

After doing the What Management Game with helping as a single focus, you can combine it with organizing, the strategy previously taught. This expansion insures the correct application of the strategy.

> What strategy—helping or organizing? (CR: Organizing.) How do you know? (CR: The girl is arranging the clothes.) Does she need help arranging? (CR: It doesn't look like it.) I agree with that prediction. It looks easy for her.

You can use many possible variations in this exchange. Help can be given to any task or self-management behavior. By pointing out such relationships, you expand your child's potential to adapt. Additionally, you add variety to what you say to the child, keeping the What Management Game full of variety. Eventually, you ask for, or test, the child's knowledge of these relationships.

> Tell me about what that man is doing. (CR: Helping the other man.) What is the other man doing? (CR: Arranging the books on the top shelf.)

The test gives the child little if any direction. The child can now see how people interact. Because of the variations that can arise, you follow the situation that presents itself, relying on your knowledge of inductive thinking and the self-management strategies. At times you will have to add a prompt to get or keep the game going.

Family Activity Planning. Once your children begin to offer or ask for help, you can continue to expand their skills within family activity planning. With almost every plan that you make, from maintaining the yard to shopping for groceries, your children can perform part of the task. As you make plans, all you have to do is ask something like, "Do you see where you could help in this activity?" If they can identify some part of the task where help is needed, you would continue by asking, "Would you like to take on responsibility for that part of the task?" If they say yes, they move from a helper to a task participant. It is an important move.

If they don't see where to help, prompt with a suggestion like, "You could carry in the groceries or help find the food in the store. Would you be willing to help me by doing those parts of the task?" If they have been reinforced for asking and offering help, they will answer yes. When they take on the role of a task participant, you may have to prompt their performance. This usually involves a little thinking ahead the night before the activity. You ask them about their plans for the next day, reminding them of their part only if they forget.

Refinement Teaching

Expansion teaching covers all the variations and maximizes the likelihood of appropriate helping. Refinement teaching insures that children respond quickly to the conditions of helping. You can do this directly during the family teaching activity, over dinner, or during any instance of helping. Here are two examples.

[During dinner.] Thanks again for offering help this afternoon. You could see that the task was hard. That is one condition for offering or asking for help. Some others are knowing that the person can't do it, that doing the task alone would be dangerous, or that you have the time and skills to help. Did you see any other conditions for offering? (CR: No.) For me, cleaning up the garage is no fun. So thanks for helping and making it a little more fun. You know I like working with you.

A little later the child may provide the opportunity to inquire about conditions for asking for or offering to help.

(CR: Can you put these pieces together? I can't get it.) When you try and can't, that's a good condition for asking for help. [Helps put pieces together.] Do you remember some of the other conditions for asking or offering help? (CR: Yes. The task is hard or dangerous to do alone. And knowing that you can help.) That's a good set of conditions. And look, the parts are together. So, helping got the job done.

From this point you can simply model why you offer or ask for help.

Henry, could you help? I would like to get this done a little faster so we have plenty of time to get to the movie.

Henry, you look like you are having a hard time with that. I think I know how to help. Could you use a little help?

When the child begins to initiate asking and offering, then you know that the appropriate conditions are setting the occasion for helping. From this point, the natural environment should support healthy helping.

The consequences for helping are the reverse side of the conditions for predicting its need. We ask or offer because the task gets completed, time is saved, work is easier, and there is less danger of injury. Additionally, there is a chance to learn how to do something. Even the helper can learn by helping a person who has a lot of skill. Statements and questions can get at these.

> [At the end of the task.] Mark, thanks for helping with the painting. I was tired, and you made the task easier and kept me going.
>
> I would have hurt my back for sure without your help. Thanks for helping prevent an injury.
>
> What do you think was a consequence of your helping? (CR: It was fun, and it did not take very long this way.) You're right, I never would have finished today without your help. Thanks.
>
> Did my help have a useful consequence? (CR: Yes. I learned how to fix the tire on my bike. It doesn't seem hard now.)

You can insert predictions about the conditions and consequences into the What Management Game by asking "Why would you help?" or "What would be the consequence of helping?" When the children begin to identify reasonable conditions and consequences and are rewarded by their identification, you have essentially completed your part of refinement teaching. The contingencies of their activities will now set the occasion for and reinforce appropriate helping.

When children ask for help, they are often asking to be taught something. Reciprocally, it is often a good time to teach. Parents sometimes offer help because they want the child to do the task correctly from the start. This tendency should be avoided. Let children explore and experiment. After they have tried for a while, it is fine to offer help. But give them the chance to do it on their own. You can talk about this perspective in helping situations.

[Child crying.] I saw you trying. When you can't get it and have tried, what have we talked about doing? (CR: Getting help.) Can you ask me for help? (CR: Can you help me with this?) I sure can. Here. [Guides child in assembling toy.] See how easy it is when you ask?

(CR: Mommy, can you put this dress on my doll?) You want my help. Have you tried? (CR: No. I can't.) Well, why don't you try, and I will watch and help if you need it. Here, sit on my lap.

In combination with rewarding appropriate asking, you have insured that asking will occur under the appropriate conditions. Here are two reinforcing statements related to helping.

Filling and moving those bags of leaves is hard. By helping each other, you showed me a fine example of following the principle of membership.

Thanks for helping me put away the groceries. How are you doing with your composition? Can I help?

The first links helping with the family principle of membership. The parent could have noted it as an example of cooperation as well. The second example shows that helping can give access to being helped.

OPPORTUNITIES FOR HELPING

Do the activities of your family system allow for helping? If opportunities are numerous, then your teaching occurs naturally within everyday activities. Helping can occur within and across activities. When two or more are working together, they are participating, collaborating or cooperating within an activity task. Yet as they do their parts, they may need to be aided, assisted or supported. Set the occasion for helping across activities during family activity planning by anticipating the need and asking who would be able to help.

CHAPTER 8

SHARING

Sharing conserves resources and facilitates membership, enabling people to get along and keep tasks flowing. Like helping, sharing embodies cooperation. There are a family of terms related to sharing. Here is a sample. *Lending* involves letting someone else use your resources or tools for a period of time before returning them. *Borrowing* is sharee-initiated lending. *Reciprocal sharing* implies having access to one another's individually held resources. *Joint ownership* suggests mutual sharing by both parties over an extended period of time. *Giving* sets a boundary for sharing when resources are plentiful for some but not for others. We "share our wealth" with the less fortunate, for instance, when we give to the United Way.

SHARING AS A PAIR OF STRATEGIES

The strategies of sharing are parallel to those of helping. The figure on the following page illustrates the steps of sharing from the perspective of the sharer and the sharee (the one who receives the tools or resources). Either the sharer or sharee can identify the need for sharing (step 1). If the offer or the request for sharing (2) is accepted (3), then the participants share as needed. If the offer or the request for sharing (2) is rejected (3), then the rejection is accepted (4) and the interaction ends. If sharing has occurred, the sharee returns the item when done and thanks the sharer (5). In turn, the sharer accepts the thanks (5).

SHARING STRATEGIES

—— SHARER'S STRATEGY ——

1. **IDENTIFY THE NEED TO SHARE**
2. **OFFER TO SHARE**
3. **IF OFFER ACCEPTED,**
   SHARE AS NEEDED
4. **IF OFFER REJECTED,**
   ACCEPT REJECTION
5. **IF THANKED FOR SHARING,**
   ACCEPT THANKS

—— SHAREE'S STRATEGY ——

1. **IDENTIFY THE NEED FOR SHARING**
2. **ASK FOR SHARING**
3. **IF REQUEST ACCEPTED,**
   PROCEED WITH TASK
4. **IF REQUEST REJECTED,**
   ACCEPT REJECTION
5. **RETURN ITEM WITH THANKS**

TEACHING SHARING

Initial Teaching

Like helping, begin the initial teaching of sharing with the acceptance forms. Once these are taught, introduce the rejection forms.

Modeling. You start modeling long before the child can talk. As with helping, you can make the modeling a little game. Sharing blocks, toys or food are simple situations that establish a chance to model.

[Child playing with blocks.] Will you share these blocks with me? I know you would say yes if you could, so I say thank you. [Pick up a block and place it.] Can I use another block? [Hold second block up for child to see.] Well, thank you. [Place block.] I really appreciate your sharing these blocks with me, so I can stack blocks. Can I use another block? How about this red one? [Hold up block.] Thank you for giving me your consent with your eyes. Look, we both have made something with our blocks. Thank you for sharing your blocks with me.

This is a rehearsal of the steps of sharing. All forms of sharing can be modeled in much the same way. When the child can talk in simple sentences, and after you have taught organizing and the acceptance forms of helping, you can begin the interactive modeling of the acceptance forms of sharing.

[With a small box of blocks.] Here is one way to share. It is done like helping. First, you offer to share. You would say, "Would you like to share my blocks?" Can you say that? (CR) Second, I would accept your offer to share. I would say, "Yes, I would like to share your blocks." Third, we would share and build something. What would we do? (CR) Okay. [Share and build.] Look what we have built. The last thing is to return the blocks [hand them back] and say, "Thank you for sharing your blocks." You would say, "You're welcome." Can you say that? (CR) That is offering to share. I can offer or you can offer, just like in helping. Who can offer? (CR: You and me.) How is sharing like helping? (CR: You offer, accept, and say, "Thank you.") Shall we try sharing one more time? (CR: Yes.)

The linking of sharing with helping will speed the learning of sharing. The last element (returning shared items) can be related to organizing. The learning of sharing requires very little that is new. You are putting things learned from helping and organizing together. Over the next few interactions, you move from prompts to tests. It will go fast because of past learning and because the child, by this third strategy, is familiar with the pattern of your presentation. You do not have to stick to the same toys, but do not vary too much. When you have modeled, prompted and tested offering, you can model asking. Because of his or her background, you can ask questions so the child models the behavior. The interaction would look about like this.

[With crayons and coloring book.] Another way to share is to ask. Since you can ask for help, how could you ask for me to share my crayons with you? (CR: Could I share your crayons to draw a picture?) If I wanted to share, what would I say to you? (CR: Yes, you can use my crayons.) See, just like helping. So now I would set the crayons where we both could reach them, and then we would draw. [Draw.] Are you done? (CR: Yes.) What would you do next? (CR: I would return the crayons I have to the box and say, "Thank you for sharing your crayons with me.") I did not have to even show you how to ask to share. [Hug.] Thank you for making the sharing and drawing fun.

You are making an important teaching step with your children at this point. You are demonstrating that they can think ahead and take an active part in their learning. It is an important part of adapting to a changing world.

Prompting. Almost from the start, you can keep the prompts to a minimum. Here is an example of minimal prompting.

[With box of toys.] Let's practice sharing. Do you want to offer or accept? (CR: Offer.) Okay, here are the toys. [Hand toys to child.] Start when you are ready. (CR: Would you like to share my toys?) Yes, I would. I appreciate your offer. (CR: You're welcome. Here are the toys.) Thanks. I would like to use this truck. What would you like to use? (CR: The bus.) [Share and play.] I am done. Here are your truck and car back. [Return.] Thank you very much for sharing them with me. (CR: You're welcome.)

The major prompt asks what role the child wants to take in sharing. If during practice a step is forgotten, just back up, model and prompt it.

During initial teaching, allow some latitude in what you consider appropriate offerings, acceptances and returns. Usually, the teaching of helping will have advanced the language skills so there is little or no problem with the talking part of sharing. Remembering to return items might be a problem, however. If returning items is hard for the child to remember, the child is usually still having trouble with returning during organizing as well. Go back to teaching the organizing strategy, and correct with prompts and consequences for returning. Then continue the teaching of sharing.

Testing. When your children can function in the sharing practice without any real prompting, they have passed the initial teaching test. As soon as they have the offer and acceptance of sharing down, expansion teaching can begin. The important test is the occurrence of sharing in everyday activities. Expansion teaching focuses on this element in the evolution of the child's sharing strategies.

Consequences. During modeling, prompting and testing, the consequences change form as they did for organizing and helping. For modeling, you focus on the child's attention to instruction and attempts to use the strategy.

> Thank you for making my teaching so easy. You are getting all the parts down fast because you are paying attention.

> It only took two days for you to get both offering and accepting my offer to share. That's fast learning. I had fun; I hope you did. [Hugs and kisses.]

Usually, these statements occur at the end of the interaction or during the sharing part of the practice—those verbal interactions that reward the child's sharing and learning behavior. And let's not forget hugs and kisses.

The above examples focus on the acceptance forms of sharing. The rejection forms would follow. You initially teach them in much the same way. The initial teaching model might go like this:

> [During sharing.] You have just offered to share your toys. So far, I have said yes. But there are times when I may not want to share. Let's say I don't want to share now. I would say, "Thank you for offering, but I think I would like to play with the toys I have." If your sharing is not wanted, you say something like, "Okay." This shows you accept that the person did not want to share.

You follow the rejection of offering with the rejection of asking. The wording would change very little. Follow up by occasionally rejecting an offer or request to share. Like helping, you can prompt the child during activities to reject sharing by saying something like, "Do you want to borrow my pencils, or would you like to work with the resources you already have?"

Expansion Teaching

You will find that the expansion teaching of sharing will be completed in very little time. Because of past strategy learning, your child has more skills with which to work, and there is little that is new.

Teaching the Strategy Across Familiar Activities. Your children will usually start to share across activities without prompting. But it is useful to set the stage. At the point when they begin to pass the initial teaching tests, you can prompt sharing across activities by simply asking them to share when they think they can.

> [Prompt.] What could you offer your brother? (CR: To use my toys.) That would be nice, and I predict the toys would not get broken. You may have to remind him to return them. He does not know as much as you about sharing.

The prompt gets sharing going, indicates that the child will not experience negative consequences for doing so, and sets the occasion for the child to help his brother through the sharing process. When sharing is completed, you may question the child about the interaction.

> How did the sharing go? (CR: Okay.) What happened? (CR: He returned the toys when I started to return mine, and none of them were broken.) He is following your fine example of sharing. [Hug.]

If the child misses a step in sharing, stop and practice it as you did in helping.

What Management Game. The game proceeds in identical fashion to helping. First, you do the game with an emphasis on sharing.

> Look over there. Do you think those two are sharing? (CR: No.) What do you think it is? (CR: Helping.) I agree with your prediction.

> Look. Could those two be sharing? (CR: Yes.) What could she have said to start the offer to share? (CR: Would you like to use my toys?) That's one clear way to offer.

You can ask the child how he would offer, accept, return, reject and accept rejection. The last of these would occur after the rejection forms were taught.

Next, you can combine it with organizing and helping. The format is the "What strategy?" question. From that point it can be "anything goes" when you ask about organizing elements, or how helping or sharing could be done. Unlike helping, how to do the actual sharing is of little importance. The focus is on the variations in the way the offer, the acceptance, the rejection, or the acceptance of the rejection for sharing are made.

> What strategy could be done there? (CR: Sharing.) I would reject the offer by saying, "I am playing with them right now. If you want to use them when I am done, that is okay." How would you accept that rejection? (CR: I would say, "Okay.") That sounds good to me. It's nice that you get to use them, but not for a while.

It is your modeling of various alternatives during the game that provides the child with models. The child is always performing at least half of the interaction. When you change it around some time in the future, you would ask the child how she would reject the offer. Elements of your previous model should appear in the child's answer.

Family Activity Planning. Once your children begin to offer and ask to share, you can continue to expand their skills within family activity planning. As the family plans new activities, ask your children if they think they may need to share using particular toys, tools, or other equipment. For instance, if your children are washing their own clothes, they may have to plan a time for their sharing in the sense of taking turns using the washer and dryer.

Refinement Teaching

To insure speedy, accurate, and consistent sharing, there are two things you can do. The first is to provide positive consequences for appropriate sharing. If your child shares appropriately, show your enthusiasm and tell your spouse about it at dinner time. Point out the consequences for sharing.

John and Harriet, thanks for sharing the blocks while I cleaned. Such sharing let me get my job done, and you both seem to have had a good time with them. Am I right? (CR: John made the fence and I did the house!) I like the way you two can work side-by-side. Give me a big hug.

(CR: Mom, can I use the scissors?) Yes. Use the ones with the red handle if you are cutting paper. (CR: Okay. [*Uses scissors.*] Mom, I returned the scissors to your desk.) Thanks for returning what you borrow. I appreciate it. How did your art work turn out? Let me see.

The statements point out consequences, as well as give the immediate access consequences of hugs and getting art work looked at. Together they will usually insure the speed, accuracy and consistency of sharing.

A second way to refine sharing incorporates a little thinking ahead and behind relative to your child's activities.

[On the way to day care.] When you play with the other children today, what strategy do you think you will need to use.? (CR: Sharing?) That's one of them. Where do you predict you will need to share? (CR: When we swing and take turns on the slide.) Those are certainly two important places. You have a good day. How about a big kiss for dad?

[At dinner.] Was your prediction about sharing correct? (CR: Yes, I had to share by taking my turn at the swings, the slide, and a game Ms. Zello had us play.) So your prediction was correct. Did you enjoy the game? (CR: Yes.) Did you use any other strategy today?

These interactions provide opportunities for further interactions. For example, the child could ask the parent what strategies he used. If the child does not ask, the father could simply give an example from his workday. This is the normal flow of a conversation. The child is given the chance to participate, and shown a model for adult interaction that will help her deal with the adult world.

Because sharing is an interaction that supports the completion of tasks, its use illustrates following the family principles of adaptation and membership. By asking your children how they feel when they have shared, you focus on the emotional consequences that result.

I appreciate the way you two shared. Without sharing the tools, you would not have finished in time for dinner. That's a great example of following the principle of adapting. Thanks.

Sharing your crayons made it possible for both of you to work on your drawings. Sharing like that is a good example of following the principles of membership and conservation. You made it possible for both of you to participate in your separate activities.

Notice that both children, the sharer and the sharee, are included in these statements. It takes two to share, and they both did their parts. After a time you can move to questions that require the children to evaluate sharing and the principles they followed.

If the child gets angry because sharing has been rejected, or grabs things from others, a correction is needed. The correction is to practice a better way three to five times, and the better way is appropriate sharing. Along with reinforcing statements and hugs, children will get the message that you value sharing. They have a choice to share or not to share. The consistency of the consequences will determine the consistency of their choice and what they eventually come to value. Linking sharing to the Principles of Family will help quicken the building of that value.

One problem that occurs with sharing is the failure to return the item in its previous condition. There is a responsibility here: to replace or repair. Ask the children what they will do if the toy, tool, or other resource is broken. This relates directly to the settlement step of the intervening strategy. Additionally, emphasize how important it is to tell that something is broken when they return it. Next, when something is broken, they should participate in the repair or replacement of the object to the extent that they can, even if only to observe the effort and expense involved.

OPPORTUNITIES FOR SHARING

Sharing only can occur if there are opportunities. You need to ask: Do the activities of our family system allow for sharing? Review your activities. Sharing occurs within and across activities. Like helping, sharing within activities requires two or more members, but sharing between activities need not be done in close proximity or time. The child can offer or request toys, tools or other resources beforehand, or the parent can offer or request them. All these options can be initially addressed in family activity planning. After an activity has been designed and assigned, you can ask if sharing will be necessary for the activity to occur.

Another way to promote sharing is for you to have ownership of many items that your children may want to use. If two children are going to do the same task at the same time, you can give them the resources—toys, tools, or other objects—requesting that they share. After they have shared a few times at your request, drop the prompt and see if they share without it.

CHAPTER 9

SUPERVISING

Family activities don't always move forward. Why? Perhaps your family members can't follow the plan, see their progress, or motivate themselves to keep going. The supervision strategy can give you the needed momentum. When you know what supervision is needed and how to do it, you support the Principles of Family. You build membership and create positive self-knowledge. Adaptation flourishes. Enthusiastic participants look beyond their part of the task to see where helping is needed, to watch for mistakes and move forward to correct them. Quality, harmony and accomplishment abound.

SUPERVISING STRATEGY

Supervising prompts and reinforces the performance of task and self-management behaviors. It carries out the plan. During a group activity, the elements of supervising can be done by a designated supervisor or by anyone who sees the need. When working alone, we need to supervise ourselves. The figure on page 97 outlines the steps and elements of supervision.

Deciding on Supervision

First decide whether supervision is needed (step 1). Not all activities need supervising (element 1a), but new, group, active and learning tasks usually do. Active tasks that have potential for danger need supervision.

Next, the supervisor determines what supervision is required (1b). Use these guidelines to assist you.

1. Supervise only the strategy steps needed.
2. Lead with questions when possible.
3. If the task can be done in many ways, let those supervised make the decisions.
4. Always look for success.

If family members know the task, little supervision is needed. Base your supervision on their experience. Too much supervision is as detrimental as too little. To encourage participation from the beginning, use questions. Ask what needs to be done next. Let their answers guide your supervision. Your family members should be allowed to decide the way something is done whenever possible. Their decisions could follow traditional procedures or new and, perhaps, more effective ways. Always look for success (and at the same time, failure). By looking for success, you assess whether the plan is working. What you learn allows you to adjust your supervision to those supervised. Following all four guidelines listed above can greatly increase the immediate effectiveness of a new, fledgling supervisor and the performance of those involved in the activity.

Tell About the Plan

Activity participants need to know the elements of the plan (2): the resources needed (2a), the self-management and task behaviors required (2b), and the consequences for themselves and others (2c). You can directly tell participants about their part in the plan, or you can ask questions about their part. Your knowledge of the participants guides how you inform them. This step is especially important if the performers were not involved in the planning of the activity. Chapter 10 expands on the elements of a plan.

Set Activity Goals

Goals help keep activity members moving forward (3). They set expectations about outcomes (products or services) and about how members should manage themselves (3a). You want members to generate the goals. When they do, they form a motivated commitment to the activity. If goals are to be realistic predictions, participants must base them on evidence (3b). Thus, self-knowledge plays a part in establishing goals.

Direct Activity Flow

To keep self-management and task behavior moving forward during an activity (4), first decide what needs to be done next

SUPERVISING STRATEGY

1. DECIDE ON SUPERVISION
   a. Is supervision needed?
   b. What supervision is needed?

2. TELL ABOUT THE PLAN
   a. What resources are needed?
   b. What behaviors are needed?
   b. What consequences are needed?

3. SET ACTIVITY GOALS
   a. What should our goals be?
   b. Are the goals possible?
   c. Does everyone want them?

4. DIRECT ACTIVITY FLOW
   a. What direction is needed?
   b. How should direction be given?

5. LOOK FOR SUCCESS
   a. What has been done?
   b. What should be done?
   c. Is there success?

6. POINT OUT CONSEQUENCES
   a. What ones are or could occur?
   b. How can they be pointed out?

(4a).The activity plan usually contains this knowledge. If it does not, exit to the planning strategy. If it does, keep in mind your family members' experience and immediate performance (4b). The guidelines of step one direct this decision. At this point, you may become a teacher as much as a supervisor. The participant may need a little modeling and some prompting on how to perform the task or self-management behaviors.

Look for Success

You discover success (5c) by determining what has been done (5a) and what should be done (5b). Make this judgment throughout the activity. It requires knowledge of the needed self-management and task behaviors. When the activity involves little self-management, you can easily find out about success. Note the amount of task completed relative to the time allotted to the task. When the task involves complex self-management behaviors, like additional planning and learning, look beyond the task product and examine progress related to self-management behaviors. When this is done, progress appears continuous, which is a great boost to keeping the activity moving forward with enthusiasm.

Point Out Consequences

Consequences push behavior into the future. As a supervisor, you point them out so all participants see their success. You base the answer to what consequences are or could occur (6a) on the relationship between seeing potential consequences (2c) and the degree of success (5c). Your ability to expose consequences depends on your knowledge of a variety of consequence types (restructuring, access and emotional changes) and their direction (self and others). How you point them out requires knowing what reinforces the participants. The more experienced participant needs a different form than the novice.

A plan establishes the resources and the task and self-management behaviors to carry out an activity. Use your knowledge of the plan, the participants' experience, and what they consider important to success, to guide your supervision. When an activity is ongoing, the continual application of directing activity flow (4), evaluating success (5), and establishing consequences (6) is usually required, even for the knowledgeable, experienced family member.

TEACHING SUPERVISING

You teach supervision after organizing, helping and sharing. Your children's knowledge of these strategies, their improved language skills, knowledge of numerous family activities, and their participation in family activity planning helps accelerate their learning of this new strategy. If your children can read, use a poster to further facilitate learning.

Initial Teaching

During initial teaching you teach two things: 1) to identify the supervision strategy steps that you or they perform and 2) to perform the steps within one or two activities. Once again, you gradually move from models to prompts to tests. The activity or activities you select for teaching should be a group activity with which your children are familiar. You want to make the steps of supervision observable. A familiar group activity does this without the extra burden of learning new tasks at the same time.

Modeling. From the birth of your child, you have modeled supervision, and he or she has imitated you while interacting with family and peers. It is especially good to practice modeling the steps of supervising even before your child is ready to use them in any direct way. By talking about supervision as you supervise in the same way you did for organizing, you improve your supervising and the identification of its steps. This will help make you a more effective teacher, and your children will learn a great deal along the way.

Use your family teaching activity to start the teaching of supervision. Begin by modeling all the steps of the strategy.

> You can organize, help and share very well, and you are improving all the time. The next self-management strategy is supervising. It has six steps, which is two more than organizing. We have to supervise many tasks, especially ones in which we work together or when the task is difficult. So, the first step is to identify the need.

What is the first step? (CR) Yes, at breakfast I supervise because we work together to get breakfast.

The second step is to tell about the plan. What is the second step of supervising? (CR) I tell you what we have to eat, and you already know where to sit and how to eat. So, do I need to tell you where to sit or how to eat? (CR: No.)

The third step is to set activity goals. What is the third step of supervising? (CR) For breakfast, one goal is having you finish quickly so you can get ready for school. What is one goal for me? (CR: To be at work on time.) That certainly is an important goal for me. Another goal is that we have a little talk about our plans for the day. So, do you remember the third step? (CR)

The fourth step is to direct activity flow. What is the fourth step of supervising? (CR) When I tell you to get the spoons and milk, to put the dirty dishes in the sink, or you tell me how to organize, you are supervising. You are directing activity flow. You keep us moving forward on the task. What does directing activity flow mean? (CR: To keep us moving on our task.) Yes.

The fifth step of supervising is to look for success. What is the fifth step? (CR) I look to see or ask if we have arranged everything, returned everything, and are on time. What is another bit of success I often ask you about? (CR: If I like the food.) Yes, that is another bit of success I look for.

The sixth and last step of supervising is pointing out consequences. What is the sixth step? (CR) I tell you if we are ahead of time, and that I will get to work on time. What is another consequence I tell you about? (CR: That we did a good job cleaning up.) That's it, and that's all there is to supervising. Can you do like you did for organizing, helping, and sharing—remember the steps and do them during breakfast? (CR) Thank you.

If you use a poster for initial teaching, you include only the numbered strategy steps, not the elements, at this point. Have your children read each step, you give an example, and have them give another example if possible. If they are unable to, you provide another. There is no need to have them repeat the steps, because they have read them. You need only do the modeling step for one or two days.

Prompting. Prompting during initial teaching can occur during the regular occurrence of the activity. For the first few days, you name the steps when needed and assist in carrying them out. Because the child has organized, she will experience little problem. The critical steps that are repeated are directing the flow and looking for success. The others can be done once; but these two may happen many times during an activity. Give your child some latitude. Later, you will expand and refine her skills. Reserve that teaching for its appropriate place.

> What are you going to start to do today at breakfast? (CR: Supervise.) Okay. The first step is to identify the need to supervise. What is the second? (CR) Can you do it? (CR: We will need to organize. We know what resources we need. Let's get them.) That's it. What step is next? (CR: I don't remember.) Set activity goals. What is the third step? (CR) Can you do that? (CR: Let's get ready and eat quickly so we can be on time.) Yes. What is the fourth step? (CR) What is the fifth step? (CR) Can you direct our breakfast activity and look for success? (CR: Yes. What do you want to eat?) Shredded wheat and fruit. (CR: Can you get the food while I get the other resources?) Yes. [Get resources and make breakfast.] Are you looking for success? (CR: Yes. We got the resources fast and are already starting to eat.) [Eat.] What is the last part of the task you direct? (CR: Returning the resources. You put the dishes away, and I will put the cereal and other stuff away.) Okay. [Return resources.] What is the last step of supervising? (CR: I don't remember.) Point out consequences. What is the sixth step? (CR) Can you do it? (CR: We met our goal and the kitchen is cleaned up, too. We did good.) And you did an excellent job of supervising our breakfast activity.

Each day you will find the child remembers more steps and can perform them a little more fully.

Testing. One day, you will realize that all you have to say is, "Can you name the steps of supervising and perform them during breakfast?" The child will answer, "Yes," and do it as she supervises the activity. If a poster with the strategy steps is used during modeling and prompting, you test without it. When the child can remember and perform the steps for two or three days without error, she has successfully completed initial teaching. It may take about two or three weeks to reach this point. Much depends on her mastery of the other strategies and her language skills.

Consequences. As the child begins to gain success in remembering and performing the steps, point out her success. During the supervising, you might want to give some short statements like these:

That's a hard step and you got it.

I was hoping you would get that step, and you did!

More complete statements or questions would come at the end of the activity.

What steps did you remember today? (CR) What ones will you get tomorrow? (CR) You are improving a little each day in your supervising.

That was an important piece of directing activity flow. Keep up the clear thinking.

That is about all there is to the use of consequences during initial teaching.

Expansion Teaching

Your expansion teaching is essentially the same as it was for teaching the previous strategies.

Teaching the Strategy Across Familiar Activities. For organizing, helping and sharing, you have asked your children to apply their new strategy skills across the range of activities in which they participate. You do it again for supervising; but because of their history, you can begin to seek out the extent to which they are thinking ahead about what they are learning.

[Prompt.] Now that you have learned to supervise breakfast, what do you think I am going to ask you? (CR: To supervise other activities?) That's it. You sure do understand how I teach. Can you supervise other tasks? (CR: Yes.) I also think you can. Do you want to do it during our reading activity? (CR: Yes.)

[Consequence—after the activity.] You supervised all the organizing and kept the reading going. You did not need my help much at all. Good supervising. [Hug.]

In many activities you will supervise one another whenever convenient. You can share the supervising. There are three things you can do: ask the child to identify the step you just performed, what step to do next, and how to do a step. Do not overburden any activity with these questions. The only goal is to have the child identify, predict or perform the steps. After a time, focus on the steps that provide the most problem for the child. Ask the child to perform the step only if he has seen you model it in a previous activity.

The most problematic step is identifying the need to supervise. For those activities that you do not participate in with your child, do what you did for organizing. This time, model your thinking about the need to supervise.

> [Test.] What are you going to do next? (CR: Draw.) Can you tell me about how you will supervise yourself for drawing? (CR: I will tell myself how to organize and then enjoy drawing. Is that all?) Yes. For drawing, you do not need to supervise very much because you are working alone and just having fun.

> [Consequence—after activity.] Did you supervise like you said? (CR: Yes.) So, was your prediction correct? (CR: Yes.) Was there any other supervising you did? (CR: Yes. I looked for success and told myself that I got the trees better today.) They are very realistic trees. I like the green leaves and the brown trunk. They look very real. What do you like about them?

Over time, the steps will be named and the reasons for certain steps will begin to emerge as long as you have modeled them along the way. Additionally, if two of your children are doing a task together, they need to be prompted in the same way. Have them agree to share supervision.

What Management Game. Use the What Management Game as you did with helping and sharing. Use four types of questions: What supervision step is that? What supervision step would you use there? How would you do that supervision step? Could you show me a better, more positive way to do that step? As you and your child see others managing themselves, you will see a lot of supervision that is violent or inappropriate in other ways. Model some better ways a few times, and they will be able to answer the questions. They will begin to think ahead about how to manage themselves and others.

Later, further expand the What Management Game. Begin to include the "What strategy is that?" question. There are times when organizing could be as easily viewed as supervising. Remember to separate the "supervision of organizing" from "organizing." If someone says, "Would you please put that over there," they are supervising the organizer.

Teaching Strategy Elements. You can begin the element expansion of the supervising strategy once your child has reading skills. You may again have to pre-teach the reading of a few words. These usually include supervision, manage, consequence and success. The teaching can be done during family activity planning. In this case, the child participates in building the supervision portion of a plan by answering the element questions.

Model and Prompt. You model and prompt by pointing to the full supervising strategy poster and the supervision guidelines as needed.

[Display poster.] As with organizing, we ask a number of questions for each supervising step. These questions help us plan and carry out supervision as correctly as possible. The supervising poster gives these questions. [Point to poster.] Let's plan the supervising of our reading activity. Can you read the first step and its questions as I point? (CR) Supervision is needed if the activity is done by two or more people, is new, something needs to be learned, or has a lot of active parts. So is supervision needed for our reading task? (CR: Yes.) How do you know? (CR: We supervise because we are a group.) Okay. Now read the second question. [Point.] (CR) You figure out what supervision is needed by following these guides. [Present the four supervision guidelines.] Please read the first guide. (CR: Supervise only the steps needed.) The steps are the strategy steps. You do not have to set activity goals if everyone already knows them. Do we set activity goals for reading each time we read? (CR: No.) Why not? (CR: We know we want to enjoy the story.) What is the second guide? (CR) A question is a good way to remind someone or find out if they know. What question do you often ask me about reading? (CR: Can we start reading now?) Yes. And I often ask, "What book do you want to read?" Now, let's use these guidelines to plan the rest of the supervision steps.

From the start you want the child to participate as much as possible. If you ask a question and he does not have an answer, give it to him. The lesson continues with step two.

[Point to step 2.] Please read step two and all its questions. (CR) For our reading activity, do we have to tell about any of the plan? (CR: No.) How do you know? [Point to guidelines.] (CR: The guide says supervise only the steps needed.) Are there times when we are not sure of one or more of these? (CR: Yes.) So what do we do then? (CR: Ask a question?) Right. And that is what guideline two tells you to do. So do you want to change how we tell about the plan for our reading activity? (CR: No.)

You may have to prompt this step a little more than done here. Pointing to or asking the child to look at the guidelines when you ask "how do you know" is usually sufficient.

[Point to step 3.] Please read step three and its questions. (CR) Do we need to supervise this step very often? (CR: No.) How do you know? (CR: We know our goal and we like to make sure it happens.)

[Point to step 4.] Please read step four and its questions. (CR) Do we need to direct activity flow? (CR: Most of the time.) How do we usually do it? [Point to guideline two.] (CR: With questions, because we know how to do it.) Yes, but we also want to make sure that we are ready at the same time and work together smoothly. The questions help us do that. Do you think we should change how we supervise activity flow? (CR: No.)

[Point to step 5.] Please read step five and its questions. (CR) Do we need to look for success? (CR: Yes.) How do you know? (CR: The guide says so.) Is there another reason also? (CR: It is the only way to know that what should be done is done.) That's right, and what is the consequence of knowing your success? (CR: I feel good and want to keep going.)

[Point to step 6.] Please read step six and its questions. (CR) Do you know what consequences occur for reading? (CR: Yes.) And how do we usually point them out? (CR: We give each other a big hug and thank each other for making the reading fun.) So do we need to point out consequences? (CR: Yes.) Do you know another way we could point out consequences? (CR)

During an activity, steps five and six often flow seamlessly together, and questions are the supervisor's major vehicle to find out about success and point it out. This is especially true for experienced participants. How they answer usually indicates what is reinforcing to them. For your children to learn this, your everyday model of supervising will do more than all your attempts to teach it at this point. Remember that success is determined by all the consequences that occur, planned and unplanned.

Tests and Consequences. The test would be to go through the supervising strategy before an activity, and have your child answer the element questions and tell what supervision is needed for those working on the task. The newer the plan, the more she should indicate the need for supervision.

Family Activity Planning. As soon as your children know the steps of supervising, they can begin to enter into planning the supervision elements of a family activity. Even for "adult" plans, you can ask them how they would supervise. If the plan involves them, they can tell you how they would like to be supervised. After they learn the supervision elements, they can participate to an even greater extent. They can, for example, supervise parts of family activity planning. You may have to prompt them the first few times on directing the flow of the activity, but they will do a creditable job.

Refinement Teaching

As with all refinement, you focus on the speed, accuracy and consistency of supervising. Of these, accuracy is the most important. To achieve it, reinforce accuracy across a range of activities, both individual and group, using statements and questions about the specific steps performed or how the supervision appeared to fit what was needed (1b).

Rhonda, thank you for supervising Jeremy in getting dressed. I like the way you often ask him if he can do each little part of dressing himself. He will get better at it much sooner if he practices.

Rhonda, did you have to supervise when you cleaned up the lawn with Randy? (CR: Yes.) Why? (CR: We are just beginning to learn how to do it, and we had to work together to get the bags filled with leaves.) You two are certainly starting to be expert supervisors. Thank you for raking the lawn and clearing off the sidewalk.

Zelda, that was a nice thing to say to your brother about how he was doing on the task.

Of course you will want to reinforce the other refinement attributes as well.

Zelda, your dad said he was proud of the way you supervised yourself and finished cleaning your room so fast. Do you think you got done faster? (CR: Yes. And it sure feels better when it's clean.)

Zelda, by supervising your own play, I had time to teach your sister a little more about organizing. Remember when you learned it? You're not only a fine organizer, but you are doing a great job of supervising yourself. That really helps me. Thank you. [Hug.]

You can easily add references to or ask questions about the Principles of Family.

When you two cooperate in supervising each other, you are following the principles of membership and adaptation.

Zelda, when you ask your brother about how you two should supervise the task, what principle of family are you contributing to? (CR: Principle two, representation.) I agree. And thanks for supervising him while I figured out our budget for next month.

When your children can remember the steps and perform supervision across a range of activities, your teaching of supervising is essentially over. But continue to include supervision in the What Management Game and make sure that they participate in planning the supervision portion of family activities.

CHAPTER 10

PLANNING

Planning helps you meet your goals, achieve rewarding and enjoyable outcomes, and overcome the challenges and obstacles in your life. By understanding planning as a strategy and teaching it to your children, your whole family can participate in influencing the quality of your everyday life.

PLANNING STRATEGY

A *plan* tells you how to get what you want, whether it's stability or change. The "how" identifies the conditions and behaviors required. The "what you want" identifies the consequences. Thus, a plan describes an activity contingency. *Planning* is inductive behavior. You first look ahead and then behind, wedging implementation between the two parts of the process. The plan is simply a prediction. Implementation gives it an observable reality that allows you to evaluate its worth. Traditionally, planning has been equated with problem-solving. That is true if you define a "problem" as something that can be either positive or negative. The figure on page 111 outlines the steps and elements of the planning strategy.

Identify the Problem

Planning begins with the recognition of a problem. Some part of your life, viewed as a contingency, needs to change. The actual problem statement (1a), "What is the problem?" can focus on the conditions, behaviors or consequences of a contingency. You may want to potty-train your child, plan a family vacation, or add an extra bedroom. The goal of 1a is simply to recognize that something extra is needed to get more of what you want and less of what you don't want in your life.

To clarify the problem statement ask, "What plan needs changing?" For each problem there is an activity plan that needs changing or is needed, but does not exist (1b). Next, you ask, "Why change the plan?" (1c) This question focuses on the consequences of adding or modifying activities. Look at the restructuring, access and emotional consequences for all family members. It is at this point that the Principles of Family begin to help. They direct your attention to the consequences you desire. If your reasons for changing the plan are supported by the principles, then continue planning. If they are not, you may want to terminate your planning. You don't want a solution that creates more problems than it solves.

Identifying both the plan (1b) and its consequences (1c) helps you avoid the trap of stating a solution before you have clarified the problem. For example, wanting an extra bedroom or a vacation can be viewed as partial solutions that limit your view. If you step back and look at what plan needs changing or why change the plan, you may discover something entirely different. The "extra bedroom" problem might be a need for changing the sleeping plan (1b) to provide more privacy or space for family members (1c). The "vacation" problem may mask a need to learn to relax more during evenings and weekends. Now both problem statements (1a) have been clarified and allow you a wider field in which to design solutions. If you realize that you want to change how the family members sleep because they need privacy, or that you need to learn to relax, then you enter step two of planning with a more accurate and less limiting problem.

Design Solutions

When you or your children design solutions (2), you begin by examining the plan identified in 1b and ask 2a, "What changes are needed?" How would you improve the contingency components of the plan? Then ask, "How can the changes can be designed?" (2b) For your children, your first goal is to work within their knowledge of activities, and provide them with experience in changing contingency components when designing solutions.

If you design other ways to sleep, relax, or do the dishes, you are halfway home. Question 2c, "Does anything else change?" requires that you look at what other activities change or are needed so the new plan can be implemented. If you are going to add a bedroom, you will not only need to design the bedroom, but decide how to finance it. In this case, other activities may have to be put on hold for awhile. You build secondary plans to insure that the primary plan can be implemented. This is "systems thinking." You determine how changes in one activity change or require others.

PLANNING STRATEGY

1. IDENTIFY THE PROBLEM
   a. What is the problem?
   b. What plan needs changing?
   c. Why change the plan?

2. DESIGN SOLUTIONS
   a. What changes are needed?
   b. How can they be designed?
   c. Does anything else change?
   d. Is the new plan clear?

3. SELECT A SOLUTION
   a. What consequences could occur?
   b. Does the plan fit the resources?
   c. Does everyone want to?
   d. Which plan has the best fit?

—— *IMPLEMENT THE NEW PLAN* ——

4. EVALUATE THE SOLUTION
   a. Was the plan followed?
   b. Were there problems?
   c. Is improvement needed?

A clear solution has been designed (2d) when the major contingency components of the main plan and secondary plans are specified. You may need to gather more detailed information to complete implementation, but your plan is clear enough.

Select a Solution

When you design a solution, you consider the consequences at least to some extent. When it comes to selecting one of your solutions, you look at consequences once again (3a). By stepping back and including the perspective of the Principles of Family, you can begin to do design-level evaluation. Sometimes a primary plan accomplishes the desired goal, but the consequences of the secondary plans are unacceptable. For instance, having a contractor build your bedroom might require taking out a second mortgage, which could raise your monthly payments beyond comfortable means. Or you might have enough money to do it yourself, but do not have the time or skills to perform the task successfully or without excessive stress. Identifying such consequences tells you that the plan does not fit the resources (3b). Your willingness to go ahead with the plan may be dependent on your family's commitment to the project (3c).

Questions 3a, 3b and 3c are part of a piece, each adding to or subtracting from the desirability of the solution. To decide which plan to select (3d), you compare your answers from the first three questions (3a, b, c) for each potential solution. Two pieces of self-knowledge can help you here: 1) the extent to which you are willing to take risks, and 2) the extent to which everyone involved is in agreement.

Implement the Solution

Implementation is not a planning step. Use the organizing and supervising strategies to implement your plan. The supervisor and activity members make two observations that help in the evaluation phase of planning: the extent to which the implementation follows the plan and the consequences that take place.

Evaluate the Plan

Evaluation begins as soon as implementation starts. The observations first let you answer 4a, "Was the plan followed?" If the plan could not be implemented even though everyone did his or her part, then the plan has some basic flaws.

When you have completed a component of your implementation, you ask 4b, "Were there problems?" This question refers to unforeseen events. Maybe two people working together could not supervise each other as planned, or hidden costs were revealed during implementation.

Even when there are problems, there may be no reason to improve upon the plan (4c). It may just need more time to work. A plan often requires new behaviors that take time to learn. A partial solution may be acceptable for now. You may have converted part of a basement into a bedroom or taken a long weekend as a mini-vacation. Your son and daughter may have had difficulty in sharing resources or doing a job; but given a little time and your careful reinforcement and correction of their behavior, it may all work out. Giving the plan a chance to work is an important rule of planning, both from the perspective of giving people time to learn behaviors and to have the consequences realized.

TEACHING PLANNING

Long before you undertake teaching the planning strategy, your children will have learned to think ahead and behind, participate in family activity planning, and know the parts of an activity plan—its conditions, behaviors and consequences.

Initial Teaching

Initial teaching brings the two phases of planning and the observations during implementation as close together as possible so that you have a better chance to reinforce planning as a process. You accomplish this through the replanning of activities with which your children are familiar.

Modeling and Prompting. The initial teaching of planning introduces the planning steps at the most inclusive levels. Just before a short regular activity, you initially teach planning as follows.

> You have been making predictions about what is needed for an activity and how to do it; but at times you will want to do things differently. To do them differently and be successful, you plan. How would you like to plan another way for us to read stories together? (CR: I would.) Okay. The first part of planning is to identify a problem. I just did that when I said it is sometimes nice to change things. We like reading together, but we could do it differently for the fun of it. Do you want to do it differently just for the fun of it? (CR: Yes.)

Step one of planning is provided; but there may be an opportunity to start planning when the child seems bored with an activity.

> So, you're having a problem. You don't want to play with your toys. When you have a problem and you want to get rid of it, you plan. Should we plan something else for you to do? (CR: Yes.)

With the first step of planning completed, move to step two: design a solution.

> The second step of planning is to design a solution, or find a better way. How are you playing now? (CR: I move the logs with the truck to the basket and put them over there, and then I lift them with the crane.) To design a solution or find a better way, how could you play with these toys? [Point to the array of toys, not just the truck and logs.] (CR: Make a house for the truck to drive through or hide the truck in. I could make a house for the crane.) Those are all other ways. If you like them, they are better ways for you.

You can model solutions by giving him the first one and then prompt him by asking for others. The key to making planning work at this point is to stay within a well known activity and to expect the child to make only minor variations. The critical element here is the use of the "better way." The child has already been introduced to the idea of better ways as they relate to conflicts (Chapter 3). Use this background knowledge to facilitate your teaching of planning.

Step three of planning is to pick a solution, or better way. Can you make a prediction about which you want to do? (CR: Build a house to hide the truck.) So, you have a plan. Now it is time to give it a try. Can you give it a try? (CR: Yes.) Okay.

As your child implements the plan, stay close. After a minute or two, ask, "How is the plan going?" If the response is positive, say something like, "Planning does help make things better. Your prediction is holding up." As soon as the activity nears an end, you begin the evaluation step.

The last step of planning is to decide if your plan worked. Did your plan work? Did you enjoy building a house for your truck? (CR: Yes.) So, did planning help you solve the problem of not enjoying what you were doing? (CR: Yes.) And I enjoyed planning with you. It was fun.

You have modeled and prompted the child through the process of planning in a simple, familiar activity. The rudiments have been established. Terms like evaluation and implementation have been left out, and the child did not use the terms that were included. These terms and their use will enter into future applications of the planning process. Here, you framed planning as an extension of inductive behavior and finding a better way.

Initial teaching continues until all the terms of planning have been introduced and your children can go through the process in several familiar activity settings. They can replan an activity like reading or dressing or eating on an almost daily basis. At this point, children may find planning reinforcing more because of their interaction with you than anything else. That is fine, as eventually the process will become rewarding because you have been associated with it and have pointed out consequences that they can see and feel.

Testing and Consequences. After several plans, your children will know the steps of the strategy and apply them to activities with which they are familiar. Your interaction might be like the following.

Josephine, do you want to plan another way for us to read together? (CR: Yes.) Okay, start. (CR: First, we find the problem. We want to find another way to read together. Next come the solutions. I could hold the book and turn the pages and read the words I know. You could help me read the story. You could hold the book that I choose.) You're finding a lot of solutions, so what do you do next? (CR: Select a solution.) Okay, which one? (CR: I want to hold the book and read the words that I know. You can turn the pages.) So, why did you pick that one? (CR: I predict we will both enjoy doing it that way.)

Now, the child implements the plan. As the plan unfolds, you ask how the plan is working. She may identify problems or make statements about other ways to proceed. If the latter happens and it is convenient, encourage the child to change the plan as the activity progresses. When the activity comes to an end, ask her about the fourth step of planning.

Josephine, we tried the plan, what's next? (CR: Evaluate the plan. We followed the plan, and I enjoyed doing it. How about you?) I did, too. So, how would you evaluate your plan? (CR: It worked.) That was a workable plan. You're getting fast with your planning and keeping a sharp eye out for how it is being followed.

That is about as close to a real test as you can get during initial teaching. You have minimally prompted the child to plan. It can take from five to ten times of planning to reach this point with a young, pre-reading child. If you have taught the child to read, you can begin with a poster that includes only the planning steps: identify the problem, design solutions, select a solution, implement, and evaluate.

Expansion Teaching

After the child has mastered the planning process for a number of familiar activities, begin expansion teaching. Use three expansions.

Teaching the Strategy Across Familiar Activities. Much of planning takes place apart from the activity task. One can plan minutes, hours, days, months and years in advance. For this reason, your expansion teaching first focuses on family activity planning. Your children can participate in planning activities for the whole family, other members, or themselves. This expansion begins as soon as you complete initial teaching.

Up to this point your children have participated in activity planning for the most part by making choices or identifying preferences. They start doing this at about the age of two and a half. After they have learned to organize, they can begin to identify the resources needed and how to locate and arrange them for activities that concern them. Following the initial teaching of planning, have your children participate in a greater range of plans and contribute to as many planning steps as possible. Reinforce them for identifying problems, adding to or thinking up solutions, seeing the consequences of a potential plan, or pointing out problems. You gradually involve them in working on their own plans.

Additionally, life is full of sudden challenges that require planning. When such situations arise, prompt your children by saying, "You have identified a problem, so what strategy do you need to follow?" At other times you can ask, "What strategy is needed?" or "Is planning or organizing needed?" The first few times you use such prompts, you may have to go over the planning steps with them. Eventually, they will enter planning without your prompts, especially if their plans have reinforcing consequences. You may need to help them evaluate the outcomes of their planning.

Your children will be learning the process of planning and the content of plans at the same time. Remember, a child's plans are not an adult's plans, so avoid evaluation before the child can implement. If you know the plan will not work but there is no danger to the child, let the child implement and evaluate it. The failure can be instructive.

What Management Game. After initial teaching, add planning to the What Management Game. At first you point out situations that involve planning and ask, "What planning step is that person performing?" Characters on TV and in books plan. Even cartoon characters plan. After your children can identify the steps, begin to include planning when you ask, "What management strategy are they using: planning, supervising or organizing?"

Teaching Strategy Elements. Adding the planning elements takes place after your children can read and you have taught the elements of organizing and supervising. Without the elements, your children's planning will not be sufficient to deal with the more difficult problems they will face in the future.

During family activity planning, you have used a planning strategy poster, read the elements, and provided examples as you identified problems, built and selected solutions, and made evaluations. These are clear models, and your children have made contributions to various plans. When you teach the strategy elements, rely on this past learning.

Introduce them to the strategy elements as you did for organizing and supervising. Simply have your children read the poster. For each element, model one example using a familiar plan. Next, ask them for another example from any plan that they have implemented. If they can't provide an example, give another.

After they can generate an example or two for each element from previous plans, you again increase their involvement in family activity planning. For example, they can begin to supervise planning, at first for activities in which they have a large part and later for any family plan. They will reach this point somewhere around age nine or ten, depending on when they began learning to plan and at what age they began to read.

> Jennifer, can you supervise us through step two of planning? (CR: Okay.) You know the step and have seen it done many times. Remember, the major goal is to get us through each question. We want to complete designing solutions if possible.

The only prompt is to mention the goal of supervising the planning step. You may have to prompt moving on by saying something like, "Do we have enough ideas?" If the poster is available, it may be enough to simply point to the next element.

Refinement Teaching

Refinement teaching focuses on (1) reinforcing the speed with which contributions are given, (2) their relevance to the problem or strategy step, (3) their creative nature, (4) the cooperative interactions required while planning in a group, and (5) the extent to which the contributions facilitated the evolution of other ideas or the final plan. The last four contribute to accuracy and consistency. You refine all of these with statements and later with questions.

> Colleen, you are really planning fast. You designed several solutions in just a few minutes. Which one do you want to select?

> That is a possible change to John's idea. I like it when you work off each other's ideas. Everyone is helping.

> Great planning. We solved that problem in five minutes.

> Notice that Celestine's idea helped Costella get the next change in the plan.

> That was cooperative planning. Each of you contributed and kept at finding solutions.

Next, you would ask rather than describe how they did on planning. You want them to evaluate their planning, not just their plan. You can have them identify how planning went in terms of the five characteristics listed above. Later, they can predict how planning will go.

FAMILY ACTIVITY PLANNING

Family activity planning is a group activity. There are a number of advantages to planning in groups. First, groups can use a supervisor to guide and prompt the activity. This allows the members to focus on performing the steps of the strategy. Second, groups have a larger knowledge base from which to generate and evaluate solutions. Third, each member's contributions set the occasion for and reinforce those of others. This increases the probability that a workable solution will emerge and that activity members will enter into planning when other problems arise.

The Process of Family Activity Planning

The planning strategy illustrated in the figure is a step-by-step tool for dealing with a single problem or goal; but family activity planning deals with multiple problems and plans in various stages of identification, design, selection, implementation and evaluation.

Therefore, I have designed a six-step procedure to help you carry out the process of family activity planning.

1. Evaluate previously implemented plans.
2. Identify new or potential problems or goals.
3. Select problems on which to work.
4. Design solutions for selected problems or goals.
5. Select solutions or new plans.
6. Summarize what planning has been done.

Starting family activity planning with the evaluation of implemented plans (1), sets the tone, reinforces efforts to date, and can add to the list of problems to work on. Only the first family meeting can't start with evaluation. Evaluation focuses on the implementation and the consequences of the plan.

The identification of problems (2) would follow the evaluation of plans. Yet the identification of problems can be an ongoing event. You can post a problem identification sheet on the refrigerator. This approach saves time during the actual planning, and provides time to think about the importance of the problem.

Selection (3) can be done by majority consensus, unless your children are very young. The problems which have immediate impact on the family, like financial stability and the health of its members, could be covered first; those that deal with improving ongoing plans, second; and new wishes, goals and problems, third.

The design of solutions (4) involves both new plans and the changing of old ones. A design may take many family meetings to complete or a few minutes of one. If your family is going on a vacation or planting a garden, the initial family meeting may allot some resources (time and money) to the project, and appoint a member or two to gather and sort out information (knowledge) about how it could be done within basic resource limits. At the next meeting, the new knowledge would be added and the plan given more detail. It may take numerous times to reach a point where at least one design is detailed enough for potential selection and implementation.

The selection of a solution (5) is usually not difficult in a group that has worked together during the problem-solving process. The selection which best answers planning strategy questions 3a through 3c will usually be selected on the first pass. When answering (3a)

"What consequences could occur?" look at the Principles of Family to determine how your plan supports (or violates) each one. This will help keep you on track in the selection process. Hopefully, everyone has represented themselves, participated, and has projects that are designed specifically for them. Consideration for individuals has been balanced with a consideration of the family. If such consideration has existed over the long run, the selection of plans is a quick and simple step.

To keep track of each problem or goal, use four-by-six or larger note cards. For each problem indicate (1) the problem, (2) the date you started on it, (3) the solutions suggested, (4) the solution selected, (5) the potential consequences, (6) date of implementation, (7) evaluation of plan, (8) and date solved.

You can organize your problems by using a note card file box with seven partitions: potential problems, selected problems, designing solutions, selecting solutions, implementation, evaluation, and completed problems. The potential problem section will just be one or more note cards that list all the problems that have been mentioned. For each problem leave space to indicate date mentioned, if found important, and when it was solved. When the problem has been found important, start a new note card with the problem and date indicated at the top.

As you make progress on a problem, move its cards to the appropriate section of the file box. Notice that these sections are closely related to the first five steps of the family activity planning procedure. The content of the cards represent the sixth step. As problems move to the completed section, you have a way to directly evaluate your family activity planning.

Occasionally take time to review what your family has done. Just a quick mention of success during family activity planning can keep motivation going in the face of difficult problems.

Planning should be done on a weekly basis, and also during times of emergency when an important plan is not working or other unexpected demands suddenly arise. Set a specific time for your planning activity and keep to it as much as possible. Display the planning strategy, the six-step procedure at the top of the previous page, and the Principles of Family. When a family member has been away from home, review the planning activity at a convenient time when the family is together.

Family activity planning should be open and airy. It is not a corporate meeting, nor a bureaucratic one. The leadership of the meeting can be shared as soon as family members have the necessary self-management skills. There is no competitive attitude among members (no one is on the way up), nor should there be one toward other families. Members work together to make their family a happy, fun place to be and evolve. You will find that meals and other family times are used to supplement family activity planning. Members may discuss how plans are being implemented, how members are doing on some learning related to a plan in the making, what potential problems they are encountering, or the positive outcomes of their plans.

Supervising Family Activity Planning

Once your family does activity planning a few times, the supervisor focuses on (1) setting activity goals, (2) directing activity flow, (3) looking for success, and (4) pointing out consequences of what activity planning is accomplishing. Any member of a meeting should be able to contribute to the task of supervising. Additionally, anyone can prompt or reinforce the supervisor.

An activity goal may include completing the design of a solution that has been in the works for a number of meetings, or getting started on several problems that all members agree are important. In family emergencies, the supervisor would not attempt to complete the six-step process of activity planning, but would call the family together and facilitate designing a solution to be implemented without delay.

Directing activity flow challenges the supervisor in two ways. First, members will often get off track, focusing on just one part of the activity planning process. The supervisor decides when to move forward. This may be done by asking for consensus or by suggesting that the family move on to another problem or activity planning step. Being stuck often comes from a lack of knowledge. Asking members to gain that knowledge automatically moves the group to the next part of activity planning. The supervisor asks, "Have we gained enough to move on?" or "Have we reached a point where we need to think about what has been said or gain more knowledge?"

Second, directing the activity flow involves insuring that the Principles of Family are considered during the course of activity planning. The principles of representation and membership should strongly influence the way in which a supervisor directs a meeting.

Finally, the supervisor looks for success and points out consequences related to activity planning. Doing so is analogous to refinement teaching—reinforcing the participation and cooperation that leads to quick, accurate and consistent plans, and the following of the activity planning process.

Family Goals

What do the family and its individual members want to learn or achieve? Activity planning should develop family and individual goals, build plans for them, and later evaluate their implementation. Both types of goals are important. They unite family members, helping them move into the future with a balanced concern for the needs of the individual and the family. The adaptation and evolution that result will eliminate much of the stress individuals and families face as they grow. For example, the stress of the teen years or the on-set of middle age lessens when you know where you have been, where you are going, how to get there, and have the support of others.

TEACHING THE PRINCIPLES OF FAMILY

You have been teaching the Principles of Family in every interaction with your children. You have pointed out the fulfillment of responsibilities and indicated rights during strategy teaching, activity planning and, hopefully, during tasks as well. When your children can read and have been taught the planning strategy, you will want to take time to give the Principles of Family special attention. First, sit down with your children and have them read the principles. Help them when necessary. After they read each one, ask for examples from your family's activities that fit or violate the principle. Model and prompt if your children get stuck, focusing on activities in which they have participated.

Second, during family activity planning, have your children predict what the consequences of each plan will be relative to the

Principles of Family. This is part of planning strategy step 3a, "What consequences could occur?" Third, have your children evaluate implemented plans. Ask them to give evidence that indicates the violation or support of any of the principles. This is part of planning strategy step 4b, "Were there problems?" Go through the principles one-by-one for both steps. You need only do this for three or four plans before your children will begin to refer to the principles without prompting.

CHAPTER 11

LEARNING

Initially, every one of us took to learning with joy, wonder and enthusiasm. When we weren't sleeping, we were learning—first by touching and observing the world around us, then by asking questions, and later by reading and experimenting. We took to learning because it offered discovery and power, knowledge about and influence over ourselves and our environment. Emotional, access and restructuring consequences combined to reinforce the behavior of learning.

Sometime during childhood, though, many lose the joy of learning. The causes are social, unintentional and unrealized. To prevent this loss, you need a clear idea of how to teach learning and how to put its process into words. When you can, you propel your children into the future. They gain a powerful way to get unstuck, to keep momentum when faced with difficult problems. Learning is the strategy of exploration and discovery.

LEARNING STRATEGY

The learning strategy guides gathering and sorting knowledge in order to solve a learning problem. The gathering occurs through observation, questioning, reading, or experimenting. The figure on page 127 illustrates the steps and elements of the learning strategy.

Identify the Learning Problem

When confronted with a learning situation, you first identify what needs to be learned (1a). In the simplest form, you have a question like, "What is that?" In a more complex form, you have questions like, "What parts does it have?" or "How do you do that?" If you were building a house or sending a person to the moon, you would ask many such questions. Learning in this case depends on knowing just what kinds, or types, of things can be learned. This is the first place learning falters. You lack a way to comprehend your learning problem. As soon as you have a way to classify what can be known, it becomes easier to learn.

The learning problem is given context and boundary by asking why you want to learn (1b). Often you are stuck during planning, want to do something different, want to make something more aesthetically pleasing, or are curious about what something is or how it works. All of these are potential reasons for learning.

When have you learned enough? When the "why" of learning is satisfied. If you plan to build a bird house or a better mouse trap, there is no need to learn all the skills of building, have knowledge about all the kinds of structures that could be built, or have an understanding of how all animals feed. The "why" provides a boundary.

There are times when nothing more than your curiosity propels you toward learning. You have no problem, and you do not plan to use what is learned. Here the types of knowledge provide a context for learning by giving it an initial organization. The knowledge types also help you evaluate what you learned by relating it to what you already know. Because the knowledge has been organized and related, it is easily remembered when you need it to solve a problem. Adding to your knowledge changes you—you see, talk and act differently. Such change is powerfully reinforcing.

Organize Knowledge Sources

The knowledge needed to solve a learning problem can be found almost anywhere: by asking people, reading books, observing, experimenting, or some combination of these. I will focus on asking and reading. The first step in organizing sources is to decide what sources could help (2a). Within the family, the obvious sources are parents and siblings. The next are dictionaries, encyclopedias, or books about specific topics. Whatever the learning sources, they need to be organized (2b) in the sense of being located, transferred and arranged (2b). When you keep a few such sources at home, family members can engage in learning at every opportunity.

Unpack Knowledge Sources

With the needed sources at hand—whether people or books—the unpacking process begins (3). First check where the knowledge is within the source (3a). This involves anything from asking people if they know about a topic to examining tables of contents or indexes.

LEARNING STRATEGY

1. IDENTIFY THE LEARNING PROBLEM
   a. What needs to be learned?
   b. Why learn it?

2. ORGANIZE KNOWLEDGE SOURCES
   a. What sources could help?
   b. Locate, transfer and arrange them.

3. UNPACK KNOWLEDGE SOURCES
   a. Where is the knowledge?
   b. What does the source tell?
   c. Does the knowledge help?
   d. How can it be arranged?

4. PACK KNOWLEDGE FOUND
   a. What knowledge is clear?
   b. How can it be arranged?
   c. What more could be learned?
   d. Go to planning?

Next, continue the unpacking process to determine what the source tells (3b), then decide whether it helps solve the learning problem (3c). If what needs to be learned (1a) appears to agree with what the source tells (3b), then the source helps (3c). The final unpacking step is to arrange the knowledge of each source (3d). Here the support skills of outlining, summarizing, or drawing graphic figures enter. Summarizing or paraphrasing are the usual methods when talking to someone. Many books, including this one, use graphic figures—often called charts, maps, displays or posters—to summarize knowledge. These forms of arranging facilitate understanding and remembering.

The types of knowledge function as a decision template, making you less likely to be confused by the specific wording of the knowledge found. There will be times in the unpacking process when a source tells something not included in the learning problem that is obviously applicable to what you want to learn. It is knowledge that is helpful in a way not previously realized. By using that knowledge now, you can alter your plans for the better.

Pack Knowledge Found

Knowledge that was unpacked across one or more sources needs to be packed, or organized, relative to the learning problem. For young children, there is almost a one-to-one correspondence between what is learned and the learning problem. One source is consulted, and its knowledge leads to an acceptable answer. If such is the case, step 3d essentially ends the learning adventure. What was unpacked is usually in a usable form—there is no need to pack it. But when multiple sources are examined, a range of knowledge must be packed together to answer the learning problem. The first step is to decide if the knowledge pieces are clear (4a). Is any individual piece of knowledge ambiguous? Do two sources that cover the same knowledge contradict each other? Are any arguments unsound or fallacious? Unclear material will have to be clarified or excluded. If clarification is needed, another learning problem exists as a problem within a problem. For the young child, clarity is not a problem. The sources, like dictionaries, atlases and encyclopedias, are clear.

Given the acceptance of the knowledge found, the total will have to be arranged (4b). As with each piece of knowledge (3d), summaries, outlines and graphs are the primary vehicles. The next packing step (4c) determines the limits of what has been learned relative to the learning problem, and offers an invitation to expand the inquiry. Even though more could be learned, the child may have learned enough to continue planning or to satisfy curiosity. Thus, the last strategy element prompts the learner to return to planning or some other activity (4d). At some future point, he or she can return to the strategy; but previous learning, other management behavior, or performance of some part of the task will have altered the learning problem as expressed at this time.

Initially, your children will not be confronted by problems that require a great deal of integration or search for clarity. They do not have to deal with the labyrinths of theory and argument that surround and direct the physical, biological and social sciences. Your teaching will be easy, because you already have a grasp of the content of their problems. You may even know the answer, but prefer to show them how to acquire it for themselves. You want them to delight in the process of learning.

TEACHING THE LEARNING STRATEGY

Children quickly come to use the simplest learning strategy: asking you a question. Teaching them a more effective (if not more efficient) way can begin shortly after your children are speaking in simple but complete sentences, and have learned the rudiments of at least several other strategies. Usually this can happen around four years of age.

Initial Teaching

Modeling. Model the learning strategy when the child asks a question about something. You may or may not know the answer. That is not important. The model focuses on the major steps of the strategy.

(CR: Daddy, can you tell me about horses?) Well, I don't know exactly how to answer. But let's learn about it together. The first thing is to identify the learning problem. What do you want to learn about? (CR: Horses.) So, the learning problem is to find out about horses. The second step of learning is to organize sources that will help us learn. Let's get our encyclopedia. It tells about horses. You know where the encyclopedia is located. Let's get the volume, or book, that tells about horses. Here we are. Book four covers horses. See, it says "H" on the side. Let's sit down and do step three of learning: unpack the knowledge in this encyclopedia. Horse is spelled H-O-R-S-E, so I find the word at the top of the page. After you learn to read, you can do this by yourself if I am not around. Would you like to learn to read? (CR: Yes!) Then, I will teach you. Here we are. Horses. Let me read it to you. [Reads, talks to child about what is being read, and relates reading to pictures.] So, we learned that .... One is .... What were the others? (CR) You just did the last step of learning: pack the knowledge found to answer your learning problem. You did just that! Do you want to learn more about horses later? (CR: Yes.)

That is all there is to the basic model of the learning strategy. An important point is to keep the encounter with the material short. Once you have read an answer to the learning problem, stop and ask the child to tell you in her own words what she learned. That is all the packing that is necessary at this point.

Prompting and Testing. Once your child begins to ask questions, there is little problem creating opportunities to teach the learning strategy. A little later, you can initiate an opportunity.

Rebecca, what we learned about horses got me curious. Should we learn a little more? (CR: I would like to.) Okay. What is the first step of the learning strategy? (CR: Identify the problem. We want to learn more about horses.) What is the second step? (CR: Organize the sources.) What source did we use last time? (CR: The encyclopedia. The "H" book.) Clear remembering. Can you get it? (CR: Yes. *Gets book.*) Let's search for horse: H-O-R-S-E. Here it is. What is the third step of learning? (CR: I don't remember.) Unpack or find knowledge. Here is where we stopped reading last time. [Reads and talks about reading.] So, what is the last step of learning? (CR: I remember. Pack knowledge found.) That's it. What did we learn? (CR) That's clear packing. And you are getting the learning strategy steps down. What are the steps? (CR: *Names steps.*) Do you find horses interesting? (CR: Very much so.) I have always liked horses, but did not know much about them. Perhaps we can learn more about them again. (CR: We could read a book about them for our story reading.) That's a good idea.

Eventually, your child will get all the steps of the learning strategy. The following example illustrates the simplicity of a test.

(CR: Mom, where do babies come from?) So you want to learn. You tell me the steps, and I will help you with them. (CR: The first is to identify the learning problem. I want to learn about babies.) Keep going. (CR: Next, we organize sources. Would the encyclopedia tell us about babies?) Yes. [Continues until finished with problem.]

At this point, initial teaching is finished. Throughout initial teaching, the child was continually reinforced by the interaction with the parent and the discovery of knowledge.

Expansion Teaching

The five types of expansions that insure the learning strategy will be used across a range of activities are described in the following paragraphs.

Teaching the Strategy Across Familiar Activities. Once initial teaching is completed, continue to tackle learning problems covering a wide range of learning topics and situations. The situations might include those that do not involve text. The learning of skills is a primary example.

(CR: Mom, my bike has a flat tire.) Do you want to learn how to fix it? (CR: Okay.) I can show you in just a few minutes. Can you wait? (CR: Yes.) [Later.] What's the first step of learning? (CR) What is your problem? (CR) What is the second step of learning? (CR) You have organized me, but we also need some tools. [Gets tools and names them if necessary.] What is the third step of learning? (CR) So, how can you unpack me? (CR: Ask you how to fix the flat tire.) Yes. The first step is to take the wheel off the bike. Can you help me? (CR: Yes.) [Mother and child remove wheel.] Next, we look for nails or glass in the tire. That will tell you where the air gets out. Turn the tire and look here. A little piece of wire is sticking in the tire. Now we mark the spot with this tape; or some chalk would do it. Next, we let the rest of the air out of the tire like this. [Demonstrates.] Good and flat. Feel it. (CR) Now we take this screwdriver and slip it between the tire and the rim like this and start to carefully pull. Can you finish? (CR: Yes.) Good. That's it. Now, put the screwdriver between the rim and the other side of the tire like this, and start to pull like before. Here, you finish. (CR) With the tire off, we look at the tube in the same place we found the wire in the tire. [Demonstrates pulling out tube.] See the hole here? (CR: Yes.) Let's look for other possible holes. [Demonstrates inflating the tube and looking for leaks.] Look. Do you see any more? (CR: No.) I don't either. So now we patch the hole we found. Here's how you do it. Watch. [Demonstrates and talks about patching.] All patched. Now we put the tube and tire on like we took them off. [Demonstrates.] Now we pump up the tire. Can you pump? (CR) The last thing we do is put the wheel back on. Do you think you can do that? (CR) You got it. All the knowledge has been unpacked. Can you pack it by telling me about the steps to fix the tire? (CR) That was accurate packing. Excellent learning. Next time, you can show me.

The next flat tire provides you with an opportunity to see what is remembered. You can begin by saying something like, "Can you organize the tools and get started?" When you join the activity, the basic rule is to do as little as necessary, reward what has been done right, and correct what was mistaken.

What Management Game. The game is used exactly as with the previous strategies. The only problem is that it is hard to observe the steps of the learning strategy that others are performing. But you can proceed to the second part of the game and ask something like, "What strategy are they performing?" or "What strategy are they performing: learning, planning or supervising?"

Teaching Strategy Elements. After your children can read, have learned the strategy steps, and have used the strategy across a range of problems and situations, introduce the learning strategy poster. Have them read the poster one element at a time. After they read each element, ask them to give an example that they have done. If they can't, give them one and then ask them for another. You need only do this for one day. If on the second day they are having difficulty providing examples, you have not covered enough learning problems with them. Wait until you have.

Once you have successfully introduced the elements to your children, start following them during as many learning problems as possible. Post the strategy near the place where you keep your dictionary, encyclopedias and other reference books. For any learning problem, you can focus on the elements of one step more than others, with steps three and four needing the most support. Eventually, your children will remember the elements. When they independently use them to explore a learning problem, they have mastered the learning process, its steps and elements.

Teaching the Strategy Support Skills. Once the learning process has been firmly established, all that remains is giving the learning strategy as much power as you can. Teach reading and comprehension skills first. After that point, anything that helps your children solve a learning problem can be included. See the Support for the Learning Strategy section that follows.

Family Activity Planning. As soon as your children know the elements of the learning strategy, they can begin to undertake or participate in the learning needed to complete a plan. You may have to work with them for awhile; but as their learning strategy support skills grow, they can do much on their own.

Refinement Teaching

Refining your children's use of the learning strategy comes at the same time as expansion teaching. You prompt and reward the rate at which the steps are carried out, the sources thought of or found that could be of help, and the variations in ways the knowledge found was packed. Additionally, reward them for seeing and identifying learning problems.

I like the way you identify what you want to learn. Let's learn about it. What sources could help? (CR: The dictionary.) Okay...etc.

You look stuck. What strategy do you need to use? (CR: The learning strategy.) What do you need to learn? (CR) That was fast focusing on the problem. Do you want me to work with you?

The first example rewards identifying a problem. The second prompts and rewards it with access to the parent's help in learning.

Once they can quickly get to the learning problem and have a strategy to get the answer, your children's emotional state in the face of needing to learn will be more calm and assured.

Additionally, you can relate using the learning strategy to the Principles of Family.

> When you use the learning strategy like that, you take responsibility for insuring your rights of health, adaptation and evolution. You can learn how to keep yourself healthy, learn how to perform the tasks that are part of the family, and undertake the learning of new activities that you see as helping you evolve.

Soon, your children will tell you what they learned, describing their process of learning and what they see left to learn. When such events happen, your children have reached a point that allows for several things. First, congratulate yourself. You did a great job of teaching. Second, congratulate your children. It is time for a rite-of-passage, a celebration that publicizes your joy. Decide just what this knowledge allows your children to do—what further step into adulthood has been earned?

SUPPORT FOR THE LEARNING STRATEGY

Reading and Comprehension Skills

Since books contain much of what your children will learn, reading and comprehension skills give them a powerful tool to facilitate learning. You can begin to teach your children to read at about age four. The exact time depends on their language skills. If they speak in clear sentences, follow directions, express their needs, and identify a host of objects that surround them, they are usually ready. There are two effective reading programs for parents that I recommend: *Teach Your Child to Read in 100 Easy Lessons* by Engelmann, Haddox, and Bruner (originally published by Simon and Schuster, 1983) and *Hooked on Phonics* by Gateway Educational Products. The first can be easily obtained by calling the Association for Direct Instruction at 1-503-485-1163, and the second by calling 1-800-ABC-DEFG. Both of these cover beginning reading and comprehension. The program by Engelmann is much less expensive (about $22) and faster, but requires stronger teaching skills. The program by Gateway costs more (about $175) and takes longer to reach the same level of reading proficiency, but it is easier for parents to use.

Besides the basic comprehension of text—answering the who, what, when, where and how questions for a sentence—there is another kind of comprehension that helps in learning: the classification of knowledge into types. Essentially, there are ten knowledge types.

1.   What something is.
2.   What something does.
3.   What features something has.
4.   What parts something has.
5.   What members something has.
6.   How something changes.
7.   How something happens.
8.   Why something happens.
9.   When something is or happens.
10. Where something is or happens.

There are several ways to look at these, but teaching your children to identify knowledge types gives them extensive power while learning or planning. For example, they can help answer four learning strategy questions: (1a) "What needs to be learned?", (3b) "What does the source tell?", (3c) "Does the source help?" and (4c) "What more could be learned?" If you sit back for a moment and try to generate examples for each type, you will have little problem.

A child's initial learning problems are of the "what is that?" form and related to (1) what something is, or the "what is that doing?" form related to (2) what something does. As the child's language skills improve, learning problems begin to cover the entire range of knowledge types. When children can identify knowledge types, the learning problem statement is clearer, and they have an easier time finding knowledge that matches.

Knowledge Sources

Substep 2a, "What sources could help?" requires knowing the kinds of things the various sources tell. Most of what you need to know for the problems of young children are found in atlases, dictionaries, or encyclopedias. Over the long term, books, graphs, charts, magazines, newspapers and journals will be important. Your local librarian can recommend dictionaries and other sources.

As your children get older, you will want to include more sophisticated sources and add a few subject matter books on people, animals, science and places. Look for those that are written so you can discern the knowledge types. If you can't easily classify what they are trying to tell you, classify them as unclear. Again, your local librarian is your best help when it becomes time to add to your learning library.

Locating Sources

The sources that locate other sources (2b) come into play once the learning strategy has been used for some time. They include librarians, card catalogues, indexes, bibliographies and abstracts. The first two are the most important in teaching your children the learning strategy. Once they can read, the card catalog and a friendly librarian can take them a long way toward locating sources. Modeling the use of the library is critically important.

Locating Knowledge Within Sources

A learning problem is a question. You can classify it in terms of its key words and phrases, or in terms of the knowledge types. These can help you search a text for knowledge within a source (3a). They provide you with classifications as you read over the table of contents, index, text headings and the body of the text. You are looking for a match among the key words, phrases and knowledge types. When these are found, slow down and explore the text for the knowledge that answers the learning problem.

Arranging Knowledge

The same techniques are used to arrange knowledge from a single source (3d) or multiple sources (4b). These techniques include generating summaries, outlines, tables, figures and graphs. Their goal is to reduce a lot of knowledge into an organized, comprehensible and memorable form. By the later elementary grades, all of these skills are extremely useful.

You will probably not have to teach the arranging of knowledge. The teaching of the self-management strategies and the arrangements of knowledge found in sources provide adequate models. As you begin teaching your children to learn, you will prompt them into arranging knowledge. Remember that most of the formal arranging skills do not come into play until the child can read at about the third-grade level.

Clarity of Knowledge

There are three types of clarity. The first is the extent to which a knowledge source can be understood, followed or used. If it can be, it is unambiguous. If it can't, it has some degree of ambiguity. This ambiguity can originate with either the source or the learner. If no one could understand the source, the source is the problem. If you want to know where Fred's Toy Store is, the answer "Down the street," without other indicators like pointing, has ambiguity that originates with the source. When such ambiguity occurs, the new learning problem is to find a clear source

For most of us, the directions "Go straight ahead for one block and then turn left and go one block; it will be on your right," gives enough information to succeed in finding Fred's Toy Store. But if the learner does not know left from right, the knowledge is ambiguous relative to the learner. If this form of ambiguity exists, the new learning problem is to learn about the content of the source.

The second type of clarity is truth or rightness. If you find Fred's Toy Store, the knowledge was correct. When you apply knowledge, the consequences ultimately indicate its utility or rightness. If the consequences are not those expected, the new learning problem is to look for new sources. Before application, we often evaluate utility by its relation to other knowledge. The new learning problem is to discover what contradicts or supports this knowledge.

This learning problem leads to the last type of clarity: contradiction. Do two or more sources contain knowledge that is in agreement? They can agree point for point. For example, both sources may say that there are three types of muscle: smooth, cardiac and striated. Also, they can agree in the sense of supporting each other. One may identify all the types of muscles, and the other can describe the operation of one of those types. When contradiction is encountered, the new learning problem is to resolve the contradiction. Children usually encounter contradiction when gathering knowledge from other persons or unclear text. The contradiction is often resolved by finding other sources to support or refute one or the other of the original sources.

In general, you will not have to worry about clarity of knowledge when teaching young children. But if they come to question what is said or read, and can give you an inductive argument for its ambiguity, rightness or contradiction, shout for joy. You have been a successful teacher. Remember that the lack of clarity means that you have a new learning problem. If you reapply the learning strategy, you will eventually achieve success. In the same sense that you improve a plan by planning again, you refine learning by learning again.

TEACHING KNOWLEDGE TYPES

There are a number of possible ways to teach knowledge types. The following represents one I think most parents will find fairly easy and fun. You can start teaching when your child is about three or four years old and continue until he or she is eight or nine. As a teacher, you want your children to classify their existing knowledge in terms of knowledge types, give new examples as their knowledge grows, and apply the analysis of knowledge when using the learning strategy.

Initial Teaching

Begin initial teaching when your child can talk in simple sentences, ask simple questions, follows your directions, and answer some basic comprehension questions when given a spoken sentence. Teach the knowledge types one at a time, presenting them in the order given on page 135. By the time your child is four, she will know what many things are (knowledge type one) and what many things do (knowledge type two). Stay within this range of knowledge as you begin teaching. Some of the later knowledge types, like what parts something has or how something happens, will require you to give more examples.

Terrence, there are many ways of knowing about things. The first is knowing what something is. My turn. [Points.] This is a chair. [Points.] That is the floor. [Holds.] This is a spoon. Your turn. Tell me what something is. (CR: This is a fork. This is a table. That is the wall.) You got it. If I ask you tomorrow if you know what something is, do you think you can tell me more? (CR: Yes.)

[Next day.] One type of knowledge is knowing what something is. Can you tell me what something is? (CR: *Points.* That is Mommy.) You got it. Can you give me more? (CR: This is a chair. This is my cup.) What kind of knowledge did you just give me? (CR: What something is.) Okay. You know one type of knowledge. [Hug.]

It is important that you ask the child what kind of knowledge was given. When the child can give examples easily and name the kind of knowledge, move to the next knowledge type: what something does.

You know one way of knowing. Can you name it? (CR: What something is.) Can you give me one example? (CR: This is my shirt.) Okay. Here is a second kind of knowledge: what something does. Here are some examples: A dog barks. Mommy talks. The bird sings. Now, your turn to give examples of what something does. (CR: The dog runs. Mommy walks. Daddy drives. The cat meows.) You just gave me examples of what something does. What kind of knowledge did you just give me? (CR: What something does.)

[Next day.] Can you give me an example of what something is? (CR: That is a shoe.) What other type of knowledge have you learned? (CR: What something does.) Can you give me an example? (CR: The boy rode his bike.) You got it. How about some more examples of what something does? (CR: I ate breakfast. I walk to school. Daddy drives the car.) You're getting good at the knowledge types.

Notice that the next day began by testing the first knowledge type and then asking the child to name the latest knowledge type. By this time the term "example" has been defined in context. Remember that inanimate objects do not do things; they only exist. But individuals do things with them. The second expansion teaching format will take care of this distinction.

Next move to features or parts, whichever you think your child could provide examples for.

Can you name two knowledge types, or kinds of knowledge? (CR: What something is. What something does.) Great remembering. Can you give me an example of each? (CR: This is a table. The boy runs.) That's it. Here is another kind of knowledge: what features something has. Here are some examples. The ball is blue. The table is hard. The table is smooth. My watch is black. Can you give me some examples of what features something has? (CR: My bike is red. The cat is brown. This cup is hard.) What kind of knowledge did you just give me? (CR: What features something has.) That's it, your third type of knowledge. [Hug.]

After you introduce the third knowledge type, you no longer have to cover the previously taught knowledge types. Expansion teaching takes care of that. If the child can't give examples, you will have to teach some of the basic features like color, texture, hardness, size and shape. The same is true with parts, the next knowledge type.

Are you ready for another kind of knowledge? (CR: Yes.) That's the spirit. The next one is what parts something has. Here are some examples. A shirt has sleeves and buttons. The table has legs and a top. The chair has a seat, back and legs. [Points out parts.] Can you give me some examples of what parts something has? (CR: My shoes have a sole and laces. My bike has wheels and a seat.) What kind of knowledge did you give me? (CR: What parts something has.) [Big hug.]

There is no need for all parts to be named. The next day or two, repeat this knowledge type. If the child can give many examples from the start and remember the name of the knowledge type, move to the next knowledge type and add the one just taught to expansion teaching. This is a general rule for moving ahead with knowledge types.

The knowledge type "what members something has" can be looked at from two perspectives: the larger group with its members (subgroups) or the memberships (groups) to which a member belongs. During initial teaching, focus only on the former.

Here is your fifth kind of knowledge: What members something has. Here is an example. Our family includes the members Mommy, Daddy, Gilda, and you, Terrence. Furniture includes tables and chairs. Animals include birds, horses, cows and dogs. Buildings include houses, garages, skyscrapers and airplane hangars. Let me name some groups, and you tell me some members. Animals. What members? (CR: Dogs and cats.) Colors. What members? (CR: Blue and red.) Now say the whole thing about what members colors have. (CR: Colors include blue and red and green.) Yes. I think you're getting what members something has. What kind of knowledge did you just give me? (CR: What members something has.) Just wanted to see if you remembered. [Hug.]

Repeat for several days or until your child can give two or three examples without hesitation or prompting.

For "how something changes," proceed like this.

Here is your sixth kind of knowledge: how something changes. My turn to give examples. The balloon got bigger. The dog barked louder. The horse ran faster. Mary grew bigger. Your turn to tell me how something changes. (CR: I ran faster. My room got dirty. Mommy laughed more. I get bigger.) That's it. What kind of knowledge did you give me? (CR: How something changes.) That's it! [Hug and kisses.]

By the time your children are five years old, they have mastered a number of procedures. These include eating, dressing, toileting, washing, making a bed, picking up toys, and riding a bicycle. There are only a few steps to each, but they know the steps and can usually talk about them if prompted.

Another kind of knowledge. Are you ready? (CR: Yes.) Okay. How something happens. My turn. To put on a shirt, you put in one arm, then the other, and button the buttons. Another example of how something happens: to wash the dishes, you put them in soapy water, scrub them good, rinse, and then let them dry. Another example of how something happens: I take a bath by filling the tub with water, getting in, scrubbing with soap, rinsing myself off, and then drying with a towel. Your turn. Can you tell me how something happens? (CR: I ride my bike by getting on it, turning the pedals, and steering it.) Excellent. What kind of knowledge did you just give me? (CR: How something happens.) You're getting it.

Why something happens is perhaps the most difficult knowledge type to teach. Like what members something has, you have to break a few examples into their components.

Here are some examples of another type of knowledge: why something happens. The dishes got clean because John washed them. Why did the dishes get clean? Because John washed them. Because I turned on the radio, I could listen to it. Why could I listen to the radio? Because I turned the radio on. John was ready for breakfast because he got dressed. Why was John ready for breakfast? Because he got dressed. Can you give me an example of why something happened? (CR: I got to Mary's because I rode my bike.) Why did you get to Mary's? (CR: Because I rode my bike.) What kind of knowldge did you give me? (CR: Why something happens.) That is great.

When something is or happens would be next.

Another kind of knowledge. Are you ready? (CR: Yes.) When something is or happens. Here are some examples. We ate breakfast this morning. You rode your bike yesterday. Your bike was in the garage on Tuesday. Your turn to tell me when something happens. (CR: I ate lunch at noon. We played checkers after school. My bike was in the garage this morning.) What kind of knowledge did you just give me? (CR: When something is or happens.)

Where something is or happens would be initially taught like this.

The last kind of knowledge: where something is or happens. My turn. I washed dishes in the kitchen. I took a bath in the bathroom. The car is parked in the garage. You slept in your bed. Your turn to tell me where something happens. (CR: My bike is in the yard. The dishes are in the sink. The cat is under the table. I am learning about knowledge at the kitchen table.) What kind of knowledge did you just give me? (CR: Where something is or happens.) That's it. You have learned all ten kinds or types of knowledge. Can you name them all? (CR) Good remembering. [Big hug.]

It is important to remember that you are teaching knowledge types, not the content that makes up knowledge types. Your interactions with your child up to the time you begin teaching knowledge types should have included the content. If your child fails to give answers easily by the second day of initial teaching, stop teaching that knowledge type and teach related content. You already know the content and how to teach it with models, prompts, tests and consequences.

Expansion Teaching

There are several expansions across and within activities. You get all the expansions within activities underway before you start the expansions across activities.

Naming Knowledge Types. You start this expansion as soon as your child has learned two knowledge types.

> Rebecca, let's play with knowledge. If I give you an example, see if you can give me the kind of knowledge. Then you can give me a statement and I will give the kind of knowledge. My turn. That is a table. What kind of knowledge? (CR: What something is.) That's it. Now give me some knowledge and let me tell the type. (CR: I rode my bike.) What something does. Am I right? (CR: Yes.) [Continues for three or four more turns.]

Stay within the knowledge types initially taught, then add new ones. Concentrate on the knowledge types that give the most problem and the ones most recently taught. Taking four to six turns is usually enough.

Relating Knowledge Types. This expansion insures that your children can produce examples of many related knowledge types when given only one. They learn to see knowledge relationships. Playing the knowledge game lets you accomplish this expansion in a very enjoyable way. You begin by giving a "what something is" example. From there you ask the child to give you an example of the other knowledge types that are related to the element given. The child would then name an element of knowledge and a knowledge type, and you would answer. You take turns.

> Melda, I think you are ready to play the Knowledge Game! Want me to show you how? (CR: Yes.) First, one of us gives an example of what something is or does, and then asks for examples of other knowledge types related to the example. Let me start. What something is. Car. What does a car do? Sit; a car sits in the driveway. Roll; a car can roll down the street. Now, what actions can you do with a car? Driving; you drive someplace with a car. Fixing; you fix a car when it breaks. Polishing; you polish a car to make it shiny. Next, what features are related to a car? Shiny; a car is shiny when it is clean. Big; a car is bigger than me. Heavy; a car is too heavy for me

to lift. Do you think you can do it? (CR: Yes.) Okay! Let's start. What something is: Bike. What does a bike do? (CR: Sits; a bike sits in the garage.) What actions can someone do with a bike? (CR: Ride; you ride a bike. Fix; you fix a bike when it is broken. Clean; you can clean a bike.) You're really getting this. Let's see if I can stop you this time. Bike: What parts something has. (CR: Pedals; a bike has pedals to help it go. Handlebars; a bike has handlebars so you can steer it.) Melda, you're good at this. You know a lot about bikes. Ah! I have one. Bike: Why something happened. (CR: By pushing on the pedals, you go. If you squeeze the brakes, then you will stop.) I can't trip you up. Your turn to question me about something. (Melda: What something is: chair. What parts something has.) I think I know that one....

You will notice that inanimate objects like chairs and cars do not have real actions, they only exist. Anything they do otherwise requires human intervention. Thus, the statement, "What can you do with a bike?" can be used right after what something does.

There are a few rules about this game that you need to follow. First, stay within the knowledge types that your children have learned in initial teaching. You can start the game after about four knowledge types have been learned. Second, the first few times you use a knowledge type in the game, use examples that have been covered in initial teaching. If you have taught the parts of something and used the parts of a car as an example, then ask about the parts of a car. Third, give a lot of latitude for the sentence the child gives as an example. Fourth, after the game has been played for a while, you can begin with any knowledge type. Fifth, when one of you gets stuck, the person asking must give the answer. If you can't, the other person wins. When a wrong answer is given, the asker gives the right one. When an answer is in doubt or there is a disagreement, the players turn to a source, like the encyclopedia. The use of the learning strategy would be required, but the learning problem has been identified.

Sixth, after a time, vary the game in any way you can come up with. For example:

I have one. What parts something has: trunk. What somethings have a trunk? Name two. (CR: Car. A car has a trunk to put things in. Hmm. Let me think. Give me a moment.) How long do you need? I think I have you on this one. (CR: Not today. Elephant. An elephant has a trunk.) Clear thinking. [Big hug.]

Knowledge game challenge. Why something happened. The car stopped. Why did the car stop? Name three. (CR: The car stopped because the driver pushed on the brake. The car stopped because it broke. The car stopped because it ran out of gas.) You're good at this!

There are an infinite number of variations of this game. You can give points, use a stopwatch and make it a speed game, play it while you are doing almost any other task, like driving, washing dishes, or eating dinner. Shortly, it will lead to humor.

Mom, do you know how an elephant and a car are alike? (Mom: No.) They both have trunks. (Mom: Really? Do you know how their trunks are different?) I'll play it straight. No. (Mom: One you put things in and the other squeezes the jokes out of you. *Gives big hug.*)

When this point is reached, you know your children are beginning to interrelate all the knowledge that they are learning. When they begin such thinking, they have an important tool for learning, problem solving, adapting and evolving.

Using Knowledge Types While Learning. You and your children can play the knowledge game for many years, but there comes a point when you want them to begin to use their understanding of knowledge types during learning. The transition is most difficult when trying to discern what text tells. Sometimes text is not too clear, or mixes knowledge types extensively within long sentences and across sentences. To overcome these problems, it is often necessary to read with your children, pointing out knowledge types. Many maps and charts (like those in anatomy) tell where something is and what something is (given by a picture with a name).

Here is how you would relate knowledge types to specific learning strategy element questions.

You have identified what needs to be learned (1a). Now what knowledge type or types does it include?

That's what the source tells (3b). What knowledge types does it cover?

Does the source help (3c)? (CR: Yes.) You know this because the knowledge types in 1b are covered in the source (3b). They match.

What more could be learned (4c), or what knowledge types are left to learn about for horses?

You will have to model and prompt for answers for some time. You may even have to use your finger or a pencil to point out the different knowledge types. Go slowly. Do not do more than mention the knowledge types the first two or three times.

By engaging in learning with your children and teaching them the process of learning, you enter a new form of relationship. Here is an example of a conversation with your children that continues their analysis and organization of what they learned.

How was science today? (CR: Fun. We learned about trees.) What did you learn? (CR: First, there are two types of trees: deciduous and evergreen. A pine tree is an evergreen. An oak is deciduous.) Did you learn about how they change? (CR: Yes. A deciduous tree loses its leaves, while evergreens keep theirs all year. We are going to plant some trees next week on our field trip.) Did you learn how to do that? (CR: No, not yet. Mrs. Gooch said we will learn the steps of planting on Thursday.) I would be interested. We need to plant some trees in our back yard.

Refinement Teaching

Two refinements are especially important. First, you want children to initiate the knowledge game. This indicates that playing the game, interacting with you, and using knowledge are reinforcing. They will continue to "play" with knowledge and use it. You reinforce their asking by playing and enjoying it.

Second, you want to promote creative answers, which means that the child puts knowledge together in ways that make you look, look again, and say wow! You prompt and reinforce this behavior when you play the knowledge game.

Can you think of another answer? (CR) I never would have thought of that one. Creative thinking!

Stumped I bet. Can't think of one of your wild answers? (CR) That's a great one!

How did you think of that one? Great!

Remember, a creative answer for a child is not the same as a creative answer for an adult. Reinforcing those fledgling attempts can lead to increased creativity in art, science and everyday life.

CHAPTER 12

INTERVENING

As families grow and change, conflicts inevitably occur. Ideally, we would reduce their frequency, duration and intensity to a level of insignificance. This book presents an overall plan to reach that goal. First, it shows you how strong, reliable self-management behaviors help avoid conflicts. When you help and share, tasks are made easier. When you organize and supervise, you can get activities going and keep them moving forward. When you plan and learn, you get a better view of your future and can effectively cope when problems arise. Next, you need an effective intervening strategy, one that identifies conflicts in the early stages, stops them, finds better ways, and quickly settles disputes. If you teach this strategy to your children when they are young, it will become an automatic part of their social repertoire.

INTERVENING STRATEGY

The intervening strategy involves the same steps and elements, no matter who resolves the conflict. The figure on page 151 illustrates the strategy.

Identify the Need to Intervene

What constitutes a conflict (1a)? In general, it is any behavior between individuals that stops the constructive activity of the parties involved. When the parties performing a task exit to the planning or learning strategies to help solve a problem, this is not a conflict. Conflicting parties may be engaged in the same or separate activities.

As soon as you identify a conflict, you must decide who can stop it (1b). In today's violent society, it is not always the person who sees it. In some situations, it may be more appropriate to dial 911 or call out for help. Initially, children need their parents to intervene in their conflicts.

Stop the Conflict

The person who stops the conflict first decides how (2a). For families, I recommend a signal like placing the right hand over the heart, as in pledging allegiance to the flag, and saying something like, "Please stop this conflict." If practiced by all family members, the signal comes to set the occasion for using the rest of the intervening strategy. You establish a convention, like the handshake and the morning greeting, that leads to other behavior.

You next decide if more is needed (2b). If a conflict is stopped in the early stages, and those involved exit to appropriate behavior, then more in the way of conflict resolution is not needed. All intervention behavior ceases. When is more needed? Here is a list of questions. A "yes" answer to any of them indicates the need for further intervention behavior.

1. Does the same type of conflict continue during an activity, or across activities or days?
2. Does the conflict interrupt the activities of others?
3. Does the conflict damage property?
4. Does the conflict put someone in danger?
5. Do those involved have a history of conflicts?

Usually, when the conflict requires more intervention, several of these questions are answered in the affirmative. There will be very few instances when you aren't sure. If you find yourself wondering, fill in the first four steps of the document card as indicated in the Document the Conflict section that follows. When more is needed, it indicates that at the very least a better way needs to be found.

Even if the disputants can stop their own conflicts and discern that more is needed, they may not think they can resolve it. Thus, the last discrimination in stopping the conflict occurs (2c), "Who should be the guide?" When children run to their parents during a conflict, they are seeking such guides.

Find a Better Way

Finding a better way increases the chance of appropriate behavior in the future. It is a miniature form of planning. You seek a replacement for the inappropriate self-management behavior that led to conflict. You, your spouse, your children, and all those involved in the conflict could have said or done something toward each other that would have stopped the conflict in the early stages, or avoided it altogether. Saying "Let's plan a better way to do this" can avoid or reduce a lot of conflicts.

INTERVENING STRATEGY

1. IDENTIFY THE NEED TO INTERVENE
   a. Is there a conflict?
   b. Who can stop the conflict?

2. STOP THE CONFLICT
   a. How can the conflict be stopped?
   b. Is more needed?
   c. Who should be the guide?

3. FIND A BETTER WAY
   a. What are some better ways?
   b. Select a better way.
   c. Practice the better way.

4. SETTLE THE CONFLICT
   a. Is a settlement needed?
   b. What settlements would fit?
   c. Select a settlement.
   d. Monitor the settlement.

5. DOCUMENT THE CONFLICT
   a. Was a better way needed? (1-6, 9)
   b. Was a settlement needed? (1-9)

Designing the better ways (as a set of possible solutions) involves all of the parties in conflict. You are not focusing on the cause of the conflict. You focus on what could have been done differently at each point in the evolution of the conflict. For example, if Jake and Zelda have a conflict about Jake's drawing which Zelda laughed at as they were playing in the living room, there are a number of possible better ways.

1. Jake asks mother for help (conflict has started, but seeking help is appropriate).
2. Jake could ask Zelda what was wrong with his drawing.
3. Zelda could have asked Jake a question about his drawing. (Why did you use red?)
4. Zelda could have kept quiet. (Don't interfere with others' activities when they don't interrupt you.)

The first better way focuses on helping, the second on the evaluation step of planning. The third and fourth focus on super-vision—Zelda asks a question to see why Jake is doing the task a particular way (3), and Zelda has no need to supervise Jake's drawing (4).

Once several better ways have been articulated, one is selected by those in conflict (3b). There should be agreement on and a com-mitment to the better way. Next the parties practice the better way (3c). Like planning, this step insures that the resources—more appropriate self-management behaviors—are present. Having those in conflict practice the better way two or three times is usually sufficient. It is important to have appropriate responses from both parties. Here is what the practice of a selected better way might look like.

> ZELDA: Why did you color your elephant red?
> JAKE: I made it red because the elephant is pulling a fire truck and tells everyone to look out.
> ZELDA: A red elephant looks strange, but that is a good reason to make it red.

By going over this better way two or three times, the children gain a model for how to behave in the future. Now their mother, who may have prompted the construction of this better way, can reinforce the new appropriate behavior during the practice. For conflicts between parents and their children, different planning and supervision behaviors by the parents are often needed.

Settle the Conflict

Some conflicts require a settlement. Step four begins with deciding whether a settlement is needed (4a). To make this decision, you start with the same guidelines you used for determining if more was needed. This does not mean that every conflict that requires more intervention needs a settlement. Performing a better way is often enough. But when things are damaged or others are hurt, a settlement is usually required. From this point, deciding if a settlement is needed depends on the extent to which work was stopped, how often conflicts have occurred for one or both parties, and how often the present class of conflict has occurred.

If you decide that a settlement is needed, you next identify what settlement fits the conflict (4b). Most of the settlements that apply to the family involve loss of access to an activity, performing a "chore" activity, paying for that which was broken or damaged, or some combination of these.

Next, select a settlement (4c). Deciding on the appropriate settlement is one of the hardest decisions any system—family, community, state, or nation—has to make. There will be times when there is no clear blame. Both parties may have to settle relative to the family. Yet two facts should be remembered. First, if you teach self-management as recommended, you will experience very few conflicts that need a settlement. Second, after your children are four or five years old, they can be involved in planning intervention activities, making decisions on when settlements are needed, and what settlement fits what conflicts. But until that time has arrived, you need to plan your available settlements and decide what conflicts they fit.

The last element of step four insures that the settlement is carried out (4d). Usually, this is done by the guide (2c), but can be done by anyone selected. The monitor documents the occurrence of the settlement.

Document the Conflict

Documenting a conflict (5) occurs whenever more is needed (2b), and is a way of keeping track of the severity and frequency of conflicts in a fair and consistent manner. Children often forget previous conflicts, while parents sometimes feel that conflicts are continuous. Neither point of view may be accurate, so documentation helps maintain a balanced and realistic approach to family conflicts over time. Complete documentation could involve as many as nine categories of information.

1. When the conflict occurred.
2. Who stopped the conflict.
3. The name of the disputants.
4. A short description of the conflict.
5. The better way selected.
6. Indication that the better way was practiced.
7. The settlement option selected (if needed).
8. Indication that a settlement was performed (if needed).
9. Signature of disputants (if possible).

If a better way is needed (5a), documenting includes items one through six, and nine. If a better way and a settlement are needed (5b), documenting includes all nine items. If there is doubt about the need for more, documenting can include items one through four. If you plan your family intervention activity as described below, you will find documentation very easy for two reasons. First, conflicts will be reduced to a minimum because your children will be learning the self-management strategies that help them avoid conflicts. Second, most of those that do occur will be stopped before a settlement is needed.

The appendix contains a sample intervention document card that numbers the nine categories to be documented, and includes the strategy and the suggested criteria for determining if a better way and settlement are needed.

USING THE INTERVENING STRATEGY

The family intervention activity is a special activity, as identified in Chapter 3. To use the intervening strategy effectively, its use

```
┌─────────────────────────────────────────────────────────────┐
│  ─────────── INTERVENTION DOCUMENT CARD ───────────          │
│  (1) Date: _____ Time: _____ (2) Who Stopped Conflict:____ │
│                                                               │
│  (3) Those in Conflict: _____ │
│                                                               │
│  (4) Description of Conflict: _____ │
│  _____│
│                                                               │
│  (5) The Better Way: _____ │
│  _____  (6) Practiced: Yes  No    │
│                                                               │
│  (7) Settlement? _____ │
│  _____  (8) Completed: Yes  No    │
│                                                               │
│  (9) Signed: _____ │
└─────────────────────────────────────────────────────────────┘
```

should be planned. A complete plan has eight components. Six of these have already been covered in discussing the strategy: What is and is not a conflict? (1b); How will you stop conflicts? (2a); What conflicts require more? (2b); What are some possible better ways? (3); What conflicts require a settlement? (4); and, What settlements are just? (4b).

Additionally, you will have to decide how you will go about finding better ways and settlements, and how you will document the conflict. By designing these family intervention procedures in a simple, straightforward way, the strategy becomes easy to use, teach and evaluate.

I recommend using the intervening strategy in two ways. First, when conflicts are stopped, you immediately find better ways and carry out the rest of the strategy. That is ‚the standard procedure—you sandwich the use of the intervention activity into the ongoing activity. Documenting the conflict begins with the decision that more is needed (strategy step 2b). A file box and four-by-six or larger cards can be used to document and keep the record. Have a few cards on hand before you need them. You can use the example in the appendix or make up your own. Section the file box into solved conflicts and those that are pending.

When using the document card, describe the conflict in a sentence or two. This is not a detailed attempt at explaining cause; just describe the behavior and the major conditions.

Jake took Zelda's marbles and Zelda laughed at his drawing.

Here is a description of what might have happened.

Jake says Zelda laughed at his drawing. Then Jake took Zelda's marbles. Zelda said he always takes her marbles. Jake said she always laughs at his drawings. They started screaming at each other. Both yelled for mother.

When it comes to hearing descriptions, give both parties one short opportunity, decide if more is needed, and then begin to document. You do not want to reinforce making excuses. You just want to build appropriate behavior. By continuing the steps of the intervening strategy without delay, you short-circuit excuse behavior and teach your children to begin looking for solutions, in the form of better ways, as soon as a conflict is stopped. Conflicts evolve, and the idea is to help them learn to see their inappropriate behavior, stop it, and move on to appropriate behavior. Eventually, they will come to stop their own conflicts from the very earliest stages and continue the intervening process if needed, or turn to appropriate self-management behavior before the intervening strategy becomes necessary.

The second way to use the intervening strategy is the "intervention docket." It is a powerful alternative that can be used to solve persistent conflicts, those that do not need immediate solution, or when there is not enough time to implement the entire strategy. It begins with stopping the conflict, filling out the first four steps of the document card, and then placing the conflict on the family activity planning agenda (Chapter 10). During planning, the entire family participates in finding better ways and designing settlements. The aim is to show that the family system is concerned with the conflict and its elimination. Over the long run, the linking of conflicts with planning results in "solutions of avoidance." The planners come to foresee potential conflicts and design activities so conflicts are prevented.

As a final step to your intervention activity, occasionally remove those conflict cards that are in the solved section. Review them during a family meeting. You will have a lot of laughs. Everyone will see how they have grown. Now, put them away. As your children raise children, they may need a light moment, something to remind them of how they behaved and what was done about it— something that worked.

TEACHING THE INTERVENING STRATEGY

You have provided your children with a strong foundation for learning the intervening strategy. They have witnessed your intervention behavior or at least corrective teaching for a long period of time. The end goal is to have them take over your role in implementing the strategy. When you teach the intervening strategy will depend on the extent of the conflicts that are occurring. The more conflicts you have, the earlier the teaching needs to be. Usually, the child has to be three or four to have the language skills to participate in using the strategy.

Initial Teaching

Initial teaching should be separated from conflicts. You have been modeling the strategy, but now you make it overt.

[During teaching activity.] I have used the steps of the intervening strategy to stop and resolve conflicts. How would you like to help? (CR: How can I do that?) By doing some of the five steps. The first step is to identify the conflict. Remember when you and Sally fought over the color crayons? That was a conflict. Do you remember some other conflicts? (CR: When Sally and I fought over doing the dishes the other day.) Yes, that was a conflict. What did I do next? (CR: Put your hand up and said, "Please, stop this conflict.") So the second step is to stop the conflict. I have always stopped our conflicts by placing my hand over my heart and saying, "Please, stop this conflict." Can you show me? (CR: *Demonstrates.*) Now, you can start doing that.

The third step of the strategy is to find a better way. What is the better way we found for the dishes conflict? (CR: Sally and I planned ahead for who would wash or dry.) Did that better way work? (CR:

Yes.) The fourth step is to settle the conflict. Did we need a settlement for the dishes conflict? (CR: No.) We have almost never needed a settlement. We would need one if a conflict kept happening, something was broken, or someone was put in danger. A long time ago you grabbed Sally's crayons and ripped her drawing. Do you remember the settlement? (CR: Yes, you put me in the corner and would not let me play with my toys for the rest of the day.) I thought that was a fair settlement for damaging another's property.

The last step of intervening is documenting the conflict. You have seen this card before. Here are a few that I have filled out. [Covers the content of the document card.] I will help you fill out the card until you can write better. But you have already signed it a few times. From now on I will ask you to tell me what to write down. We will have to work together on documenting until you can do it yourself.

On the second day of initial teaching, go over other conflicts. If the child is older and can read, a posting with the five steps can be used. When the child can name the five steps and provide examples of conflicts, better ways, and realistic settlements, initial teaching ends. It will most likely take three or four initial teaching sessions to achieve that point, depending on the age, planning and conflict background of the child.

Expansion Teaching

If you have followed the teaching of self-management up to this point, you will be experiencing few conflicts. Fewer yet will require a settlement. Expansion teaching focuses on letting your children work on eliminating their conflicts.

Teaching the Strategy Across Familiar Activities. When conflicts do occur, strengthen the intervention behavior by prompting the steps of the strategy. Begin by asking, "Are we (or you two) having a conflict?" If it is a conflict, prompt them through the steps, and reward remembering and finding better ways. Additionally, you may ask the "Are we having a conflict?" question when none is occurring.

Are you two having a conflict? (Children: No.) Good. How about a hug for great playing.

[Doing the dishes.] Are we having a conflict? (CR: No. I know what you will ask, "What kind of conflict could we have?") Are my games so plain? (CR: I am getting better at them. If you refused to do your part, we would have a conflict.)

If you have a conflict with your children, ask them what strategy is needed. From that point, prompt as much as needed to complete the strategy. If there is no resolution, place the conflict on the intervention docket. By teaching your children the other self-management strategies, few of these opportunities will arise.

What Management Game. Our world is full of conflicts—in stores, in schools, on TV, almost anywhere people interact. The What Management Game works exactly as it did for the other strategies.

What is that, conflict or not a conflict? (CR: Conflict.) So, what strategy? (CR: Intervening.) Let's watch to see what they do. [Watches.] Did they stop the conflict? (CR: Yes.) How? (CR: The man walked away.) So, did they find a better way? (CR: No.) What could have been a better way? (CR: The man could have stayed behind that woman in line.) If something like that would have happened at home, like not taking your turn, would it have required a settlement? (CR: No.) Why? (CR: It does not happen often, nothing was broken, and no one was put in danger.)

Later you may simply ask your children to watch an interaction and ask them what they see. If it is a conflict, ask them to talk about it in terms of the intervening strategy.

Jake, see if you can find some conflicts while we are in the store. [At the store.] Do you see any conflicts? (CR: No.) Is that a conflict? [Points.] (CR: Yes.) How do you know? (CR: They are not getting along.) What would be a better way? (CR: They could tell themselves they have a conflict and write it down and settle it later. They could hug!) Those are possible better ways. I have one....

[At the zoo.] What do you see over there? [Points.] (CR: The bears are having a conflict. They are hitting each other and biting.) What would be a better way? (CR: I don't know.) I don't either. I don't know what caused it, and I don't think bears resolve conflicts except by winning and losing a fight.

If the child had a conflict at school, for example, have him describe what happened, whether he followed the strategy, what some other better ways would have been, or what he could have done if he did not follow the strategy. Asking about situations in normal conversation should be enough to keep the behavior alive and functional.

Teaching Strategy Elements. Teaching the elements of intervening proceeds as it did for the planning and learning strategies. After your children can read and you have done a number of expansions across and within activities, you can introduce the full strategy with a poster like the one in the appendix. Use these three steps: 1) They read the poster, and you ask them if they can give an example of the element in an intervention they experienced; 2) If they can't, give them an example and ask for another; 3) If they still can't give you an example, give them one more and move to the next element. You need to do this for only one day if your children can provide examples. If on the second day they have problems giving examples, you need to concentrate on expansions across and within activities for a while longer.

Once you have successfully introduced the elements to your child, start to include them in the other expansions. Use the poster to help them remember the elements. The pocket-sized strategy cards, described in Chapter 13 and presented in the appendix, can be used.

Your children may have trouble finding settlements and settlements that fit. You can deal with this problem by planning settlements during family activity planning. As a group, you identify a range of conflicts, determine possible settlements, and then fit the settlement to the conflict. There is no right answer except the one the family decides on. Usually, children will vote for settlements that you may see as extreme. They are especially prone to this if they have been the "victim." To help moderate their selection of settlements, remind them that the family can always replan if the settlement does not help eliminate the conflict. Only implementation allows you to evaluate the worth of the settlement in eliminating future conflicts.

Family Activity Planning. Preventing conflicts can be approached during activity planning by asking your children if they foresee conflicts arising during the implementation of a plan. Does the plan contain potential punishing consequences? If they think of things that could go wrong, you can have them build a plan that would avoid them, or pre-plan how they would intervene if such a conflict did occur. Pointing out conflicts that were not seen during previous planning reinforces the building of future plans that avoid them.

Refinement Teaching

As your children come to identify conflicts and perform the steps and elements of the intervening strategy, your statements and questions should reinforce them for it. You want to reinforce them for catching conflicts in the early stage (latency), quickly selecting better ways and settlements, and implementing them with accuracy. Part of the accuracy is thinking up unusual but appropriate better ways and settlements. This can be prompted by asking them to add, modify, change or delete parts of previous better ways or settlements. The key is not to evaluate suggestions. Here are some examples of refinement prompts and consequences.

Remember, you can change the parts of past settlements. What are some other possible settlements? (CR: Give me 15 minutes in the corner.) That is different. Let's try for some more. (CR: I could do his dishes tonight.) I like the way you are contributing to settlements that cost you something. You're seeing how you could change. [Hug.]

I didn't see that conflict. Your eyes are sharp and accurate. Fast identification of conflicts.

This is the first time you two have stopped your own conflict. Thank you. I know that is hard. [After documenting.] I think stopping your own conflict just as it started deserves a special treat. There are some wonderful oranges in the refrigerator. How about one? (Rose and Tom: Please!) [Later, at dinner with spouse.] You should have seen how fast Rose and Tom stopped their conflict over toys this afternoon....

The last statement focuses on the evolution of behavior, and shows the way in which the behavior can receive multiple reinforcements.

Quickly, accurately and consistently performing the intervening strategy leads to some important consequences. These consequences can be linked to the Principles of Family.

When you can avoid or stop your own conflicts, you insure your rights to health, representation and, most certainly, justice.

When your children reach this point, they are ready for another rite-of-passage as outlined in Chapter 13.

AVOIDING CONFLICTS

Your children come into the world crying, suckling, stretching and kicking. From these early moments you manage their eating, sleeping, toileting and dressing—the major activities of their lives. This management continues for the first two or more years. It is also the time when you teach them to live within the family system. Well before they learn to perform these activities on their own, they learn to attend, follow directions, and cooperate as you direct them. In other words, the first thing they learn is to manage themselves as they are being helped in their everyday lives.

Many parents fail at these first teachings. As a result, their children learn to manage the situation. They cry, whine, kick, push or shove, and the parent gives them what they want to eat, or holds them when they want to be held, regardless of the time of day or night. As they learn to walk and talk, they learn to control the activities of their parents and get their way in slightly more sophisticated ways. Eventually, the interactions of these parents and children will be classified as conflicts—the parents' activities are stopped. The emotional consequences build, and eventually the conflicts escalate. To avoid conflicts from the start, you want to be successful at your first teachings. Everything said in this book about teaching your child applies. Yet, a few additional points may help you focus your teaching efforts. Here are six.

One, plan each of these initial activities—for the child's health and yours. You have another life. You work, take exercise, help family and friends, and need some time to yourself, to name just a few. Your children have to learn to eat and sleep around your schedule. They have to eat what is good for them. They have to sleep enough for a healthy body. They should let you clean and dress them without fuss and fight.

Two, determine just what is appropriate behavior for these activities. What constitutes appropriate eating, sleeping, dressing and toileting behavior given what you have taught them? Any number of good books cover these behaviors. You will usually find, with some variation, that after six to eight weeks of age a child can sleep through the night and be fed on a fairly regular schedule.

Three, determine what conditions will prompt or support the desired behavior. Is the room warm enough to facilitate sleep? Does singing and stroking before and during toileting calm the child? Does placing the child in a comfortable position and using a soft voice help the child during eating and dressing?

Four, determine how you will correct inappropriate behavior. If the child cries instead of sleeps, what will you do (given that you know that he is not sick, is warm enough, and has been fed)? If the child refuses to eat at meal time, what will you do? If the child doesn't cooperate during dressing, what will you do? My answer to parents with these and similar problems is to make sure the natural consequences of the activity occur. That usually amounts to not eating (though given several opportunities), the child stays dirty, or the child is ignored (but not unobserved) for some period of time.

Five, determine what you will do when the child behaves appropriately during these activities. How will you treat the child when he stops crying and goes to sleep? How will you reward the child during and after eating, sleeping, dressing and toileting? You can continue to sing to him and talk softly about how he is doing (he doesn't need to understand), give him hugs and kisses, or move him through space in ways that make him smile and giggle.

Six, follow your plan consistently and persistently. Persistently means give the consequences of the plan time to work. There is no one right plan. Many variations will work, but all will take time. The child may cry for three hours before she stops and goes to sleep, and may do so for several nights. The child may miss a meal or two now and then. From an early point, however, she will live cooperatively within your family system. Consistently means always follow procedure, but not blindly. Always keep an eye open for a change in conditions—the entry of sickness, pain and hunger for the most part.

As children grow and you begin to teach them to eat, dress, sleep and toilet themselves, their activities change. They take on a larger share of the task and its management. As this happens, you will have to replan these activities. If your child does not get dressed on time once she knows how to dress, and you know she can do it in the time frame allotted, what will the consequence be? You can take her in her semi-dressed form. Maybe her feet get cold or she enters the restaurant in her pajamas. These are the "natural consequences." Use them. The child is not yet old enough to run the family system. You are the manager until you have taught them to be managers. This book is about moving your children from those who need to be managed to those who can manage themselves.

CHAPTER 13

THE FAMILY SYSTEM

One objective remains: to insure that your family functions as a self-managed system. To achieve this objective, you do two things. First, you want to teach your children to use their self-management skills as a system. Second, plan your teaching and establish a family environment that prompts and reinforces you as a teacher and your family as a harmonious system of members. In showing you how to achieve the latter, this chapter summarizes what has been said in previous chapters about teaching.

TEACHING THE SYSTEMS VIEW

Teaching your children the systems view begins after they can read and you have initially taught all the strategies. By this time, you have already modeled the self-management strategies as a system during family activity planning. Moreover, you have been prompting the use of the strategies by asking questions like these.

Zelda, what strategy should you be using here?

Do you need to help or share?

Is this the time for planning or supervising?

Zelda, what should you do now?

How should you manage yourself now?

All such questions prompt the selection of a self-management strategy that fits the situation. Given that it is done with all the strategies and across a range of activities, children will manage themselves systematically. But they will not yet be able to talk about their self-management behavior at the systems level. As a consequence, they will not be able to solve their more complex management problems by communicating with others, or by systematically building a plan that has a good chance of solving them. The systems view helps children (and adults) think ahead about the components of a plan and what strategy will come next.

Initial Teaching

The initial teaching of the systems view follows the same pattern as all the strategies. You first model the system.

> You have learned all of the self-management strategies. Can you name them? (CR) All of those strategies work together. [Display the poster of the self-management system.] They form a system. What do they form? (CR: A system.) Now, let me show you how they work together. First, you start with planning. If you think the plan will work, you move to organizing and supervising, and you use helping, sharing and intervening when they are needed. [Point out this movement by following the arrows on the poster.] If you are having problems with your plan and you don't think it will work, you go to the learning strategy. When you are done learning, go back to planning and complete your plan. When you think it will work, you implement it by organizing and supervising. You only help, share or intervene when you need to. Now you tell me how the self-management strategies work together. (CR)

The next day you would repeat this introduction and again ask the child to repeat how the strategies work as a system. For the next several days, ask her to explain how the strategies work as a system, using the poster. Finally, remove the poster and only take it out if she needs prompting. When she can do it correctly for two days, initial teaching is over. After the first day, don't take more than two or three minutes on this teaching.

Expansion Teaching

The only expansions are two modifications of the What Management Game. For the first, you now ask your children, "What self-management system strategy do you predict would work here," or "What self-management system strategy should we plan next?" You would continue the What Management Game as usual.

The second modification requires you to reverse your approach to the game. In the past they have identified what strategy or strategy step they needed to use, or what strategy or strategy step others were performing. Now, you want them to identify their ongoing management behavior and predict where other similar behavior could be used. To insure success, some models will be needed.

This is exactly how you will need to wait in line for lunch at school. It will get you to your food the fastest.

Staying next to me as we walk through the store is how you should walk with me when we go to the fair next week.

Sharing your crayons with your sister is how you will have to share in school. It will help everyone get done with their task.

[Driving car.] Telling me you have to go potty before you get desperate is what you need to do on our vacation next week.

You can begin such models at any time in the teaching of the self-management strategies. You are modeling thinking ahead with analogous evidence. Notice that either the behavior or the strategy can be described. A little later you would move to questions.

I like the way you are helping me. Where else would you predict you would use the helping strategy? (CR: When I play with Mildred.) When would you use it? (CR: When we push each other on the swings.) You are sure seeing where helping can be used.

[Later.] Did you get to use the helping strategy with Mildred? (CR: Not today, but we shared chalk when we were drawing on the sidewalk.) I saw the brightly colored picture you two were drawing. What did you have the most fun drawing? (CR)

This interaction is just inductive behavior about strategies and activities. To bring in the systems view, all you have to do is begin the above interaction with the question, "What system strategy are you using?," or in some cases, "What system strategy are we using?" By replacing "I like the way you are helping me" with the systems question, you are requiring the child to analyze her ongoing self-management behavior and then extend it into the future. Of course, you can put these two parts back-to-back when eating dinner, walking or driving somewhere. Whenever you are reviewing how she managed herself on any particular day, you can ask her to predict where else such management behavior would work.

To perform this expansion, you will have to think ahead a little about how your children's present world of activities will expand. Initially, the list is not long. How they supervise themselves waiting for dinner is the same as how it can be done at a restaurant or a friend's house. Riding in your car is done the same way in a school bus. Walking around the store and not bumping into others is the same as walking at home. Following directions, asking for help, or sharing are all done the same way, as are organizing your work, supervising yourself, and planning what you will do next. When your children see places where appropriate management is needed, they are avoiding potential problems. When they plan, they can build solutions of avoidance or prevention.

PLANNING YOUR TEACHING

There is no perfect sequence for, time to, or speed at which to teach your children the self-management strategies. There are many effective ways. All of them are controlled by what you know about your child, your available time, and the opportunities your family activity system provides for performing the strategies. Yet several guidelines help make your teaching manageable and effective.

1. Begin teaching the strategies when your children can speak in simple sentences and identify a host of objects and actions in their surrounding environment.

From the beginning, you teach them to be members of your family system. Teaching the strategies usually can begin around age four. You can accelerate their readiness to learn by providing your children with a stimulating learning environment.

2. Initially teach one strategy at a time in the order presented in this book.

You begin with thinking ahead and behind, and move to organizing and the other strategies as indicated in Chapters 5 through
12. You finish initial teaching with the systems view. Shortly after
you begin the expansions across activities, you can begin to initially
teach the next strategy. Since helping and sharing have four forms,
start with the acceptance forms for both before moving to the
rejection forms. Because of the similarity of the two, sharing will
proceed faster than helping. If your children learn to read before
you finish the initial teaching of all the strategies, you can use a
poster that includes only the steps and not the elements of the
strategy for awhile until they are ready for the complete poster.

You follow the order presented in this book because it best fits
the child's intellectual development and everyday needs. Thinking
ahead and behind gives a foundation for all the strategies. Organizing, helping, and sharing are needed in everyday life before
supervising and planning. And learning and intervening are usually
harder than supervising or planning for most children to learn.

3. Start expansion teaching right after initial teaching.

Since you continue expansion teaching for a long time, expect to
be prompting and reinforcing the use of many strategies on any
day. There are three expansions that come into play at this time.
First, you insure that the strategy is used across several of the children's activities. Second, you help them see where the strategies
could or are being used. You use the What Management Game to
achieve this end. Third, you include the use of their knowledge of
the strategy in family activity planning. All of these are going on
continually. Different days and different activities may focus on
one strategy or another, but over the long run—and I am talking
years here—all strategies will be expanded as equally as possible, or
as the need demands.

The only thing left out has been the learning strategy support
skills, filling out the intervention document card, and the element
expansions for organizing, supervising, planning, learning, and
intervening. Teaching the knowledge types can begin almost any
time after the introduction of several strategies, or just after you
have initially taught the learning strategy. Many of the other support skills, filling out the intervention document card, and the

strategy elements will have to wait until the child can read. The fourth guideline addresses when to teach strategy elements.

4. Begin teaching strategy elements after all strategies have been initially taught and the child can read.

This guideline further helps you manage your teaching. There are five strategies with elements: organizing, supervising, planning, learning, and intervening. You can teach them in the order presented in the book—the recommendation—or change them as you see the need. The better the child can read, the faster your teaching and your child's learning will proceed.

5. Refinement teaching occurs along with expansion teaching.

You begin to focus on accuracy, speed and consistency of strategy application as soon as expansion teaching begins. Your children's self-management skills continue to be refined over the course of their lifetime because of the consequences it brings to their lives.

6. You can change your teaching plan.

You may accelerate, slow down, or teach the strategies in a different order. The only objective is to teach effectively and to plan before you jump into doing it. One of the most important parts of that plan is to identify the activities in which your child presently, and in the near future, can use the strategy being taught. As you see your child learn and apply the strategies, and witness the quality of your relationship with her or him, you will most likely make changes. Many of these changes will be to insure guideline seven.

7. Teach so your child loves every minute of it.

If learning to manage themselves leads to positive emotional, access, and restructuring consequences, your children will love being taught. Your statements and questions add to and make these consequences visible. Children who do not want to learn are not finding it reinforcing. Your consequences make it so. Pushing your children to learn will only turn them away from it. Pull them gently with positive consequences and push them gently by getting them to think ahead. Eventually, the learning will result in its own rewarding consequences.

This book was written from a developmental perspective. What I am about to say applies to older children of about seven to nine years who follow your directions, offer to and ask for help now and then, do a few tasks around the house without much problem, and enjoy spending time with you.

8. To teach the older child who can read, begin with participation in the family planning activity and present the systems view of the self-management strategies.

In teaching this older child, you begin with reading this book, outlining your family activities as described in Chapter 3, starting family activity planning, and posting the self-management strategy and systems view posters. The child participates in activity planning from the start, making whatever planning contributions he or she can. Your teaching activity begins with an introduction to the systems view of the strategies. From that point you can initially teach the strategies in an order of the child's choosing. Posters that include only the strategy steps are used for initial teaching. The expansions across and within activities proceed essentially as described in the strategy chapters, as does refinement teaching. Teaching your children to think ahead and behind is overlaid onto all activities. You begin to talk to them as suggested in Chapter 5.

Throughout this time, the planning activity remains central—this older child, from the earliest possible point, should begin to build and evaluate plans. If you make planning reinforcing through the use of positive consequences, you will find that the child will begin to inquire about the strategies. It is this inquiry that can also direct your teaching.

BUILDING A SUPPORTIVE ENVIRONMENT

To succeed in creating a responsible, self-managed family, you will need a supporting and rewarding environment. You can create one by doing five things.

Establish and Use a Time for Teaching and Planning

There is nothing more important than setting aside a consistent time for teaching and planning. For teaching, a daily time of fairly consistent length is important. This is your family teaching activity. For planning, a weekly family meeting is suggested.

You can teach your children self-management skills in about ten or fifteen minutes per day. Much of your teaching will occur during your regular family activities. Get into a routine while your children are young. Start when you begin to teach eating, dressing, and toileting. During strategy teaching, much of your teaching will involve performing activities with an emphasis on self-management. The important point is that no matter what the details of your teaching or your approach to it, plan the time, select the activities, and try to follow guideline seven: teach so your child loves every minute of it.

Use Strategy and Teaching Posters

You have seen examples of posters, called figures, throughout this book. Placing them in the family environment is important for two reasons. First, they prompt your teaching and spur your evaluation. Second, they prompt your own and your children's self-management behavior. There are a number of different posters and options for their use. All the posters are presented in the appendix, starting on page 177, for easy photocopying.

The first three posters cover self-management, the Principles of Family, and teaching (pages 179, 181, 183). The self-management poster includes the strategy steps and a model of the system. The teaching poster outlines all that was said about teaching in Chapter 4. It defines what teachers do, their tools and their procedures. Additionally, you might want to outline your teaching plan. Post all in prominent places, like the kitchen, where you do family activity planning, in your children's bedroom, in the bathroom, or any combination of these. For a prominent place like the kitchen or activity planning area, take the first three to your local copy center and expand to something like 11 by 17 or 20 by 28 inches, and laminate or frame. You want everyone to be able to read them from a distance. Read them every day. Eventually, you will be able to close your eyes and read them to yourself.

The next nine posters (pages 185-201) outline the individual self-management strategies, the inductive thinking process, and the knowledge types. You will notice that the knowledge types are placed in four groups. These correspond to the four basic forms of knowledge about our world: existential, locational, hierarchical and historical. Each of the ten knowledge types discussed in Chapter 11 falls into one of these four groups.

Enlarge these nine to about 8 by 10 inches. Place the learning strategy and knowledge types posters in your children's learning areas, near the bookcase, where you and your child read together, or some combination of these. Place the intervening strategy in the kitchen or anywhere that you can easily access it. The others can be used as your children learn a particular strategy.

The next item is not a poster, but the intervention documentation card in a four-by-six format (pages 203-204). The steps of documenting are numbered, and the reverse side of the page presents the intervening strategy and the suggested criteria for deciding if a better way and a settlement are needed. Together they should help you document any conflict and carry out the intervention process. Copy the sides back-to-back on note-card-weight paper.

The final displays (pages 205-208) include wallet-sized copies of all the posters discussed above. Notice that the reverse page is the other side of these wallet-sized copies and contains related information. For example, the helping strategy has the sharing strategy on the reverse side (pages 205 and 206). The supervision strategy has the supervision guidelines on the reverse side (pages 207 and 208). The opposite side of the learning strategy contains the knowledge types (pages 207 and 208).

If you copy these back-to-back, you have a two-sided, wallet-sized poster. Make several copies of these for yourself and your children. Print on heavy card stock or laminate in plastic if you like. Put them in every place you can think of. Use the learning strategy as a book mark and place several other copies in the children's bookcase. Put a full set of strategies in the car. Keep the strategies you are focusing your teaching on in your pocket (at least until you have them memorized). Tape a set on your children's desk, and give them a set for school and to carry around like baseball cards. You may even find them quizzing each other and using them to play the knowledge game. All these posters are available in a variety of colors and sizes. See the beginning of the appendix or the About the Author section at the end of the book.

Evaluate Your System

You evaluate your system in terms of the success of your plans, the insignificance of your need to intervene, and the outcome of your teaching. There will be restructuring, access, and emotional consequences from these areas for all family members. I have covered the evaluation of planning and intervening in Chapters 10 and 12, but a few more words on them and the evaluation of teaching are necessary. You may often get lost in the moment, forgetting about what has been done. As a result, your lack of immediate success can be disappointing. But with a way to evaluate and look back on your system, you can maintain a high level of enthusiasm and an accurate perspective.

First, you have documented your family's conflicts and plans. What you need is to make a monthly summary of completed plans, successful plans, projects moved forward, and conflicts that occurred and were settled. Post this calendar of success. If you want some summary statistics for conflicts, divide the number of days with conflicts by the number of days of the month, and you get the percent of days with conflicts. How many should you have and still feel success? There is no magic number. But you should not expect the number to be zero. Trends can be a barometer of family happiness and success.

Second, keep a summary of your teaching. Do this by taking your teaching plan and checking off when you have essentially finished each procedure of teaching. Make a teaching plan for each child. The extent to which they have mastered any of the strategies is dependent on the range of activities where opportunities to perform them exist. If you check off behavior which indicates strategy performance across the range of activities your children participate in, then they have demonstrated mastery. Make the range decision beforehand, but expect to modify it. As you move from strategy to strategy, your ability to make this distinction will improve. After your children learn to plan, they can participate in this criterion-making once the initial teaching of the strategy is complete. One of the criteria should require children to state each of the steps and elements of the strategy and explain through example what they mean. An important part of self-management is having a language with which to talk about self-management skills, and posters will not always be around to prompt that language.

Celebrate Your Systems' Success

At each point that your children demonstrate their mastery of an individual strategy and eventually the system, it is time to celebrate your teaching, your children's learning, and your family's self-management success. Minimally, your children should be given the chance to manage themselves and/or others in ways not previously allowed or even possible. Frame an award certificate at each of these times and put it on a wall below an 8 by 10 inch poster of the strategy. Place it in the child's room or in a prominent place. Better yet, let the child decide. When the child has mastered the strategy system, decide what master award, rights, and responsibilities he or she gains. There is no right answer for these decisions. They depend on your family activities, the resources of your system, and what your child would find reinforcing.

Establish Parent Groups

Community, school and neighborhood self-management parenting groups provide support in learning, teaching and evaluating self-management skills. It is like having an outside consultant help you solve your problems. You will in turn consult with others and, in doing so, learn much more about what you are doing.

These parent groups are possible because you have specific things to learn, teach, and evaluate. The products are visible and enjoyable. Whenever groups are formed with a clear knowledge base and procedures, they flourish. You may have noticed that you enjoy doing almost anything at which you are a success. You can insure your enjoyment as a family member if you build an environment that supports success.

APPENDIX

The posters in this appendix may be photocopied for personal use as described in Chapter 13. You can obtain them in various sizes and colors by contacting the author at (800) 729-6094.

SELF-MANAGEMENT

Viewed as a Set and a System of Strategies

SELF-MANAGEMENT STRATEGIES

The Strategies and Their Component Steps

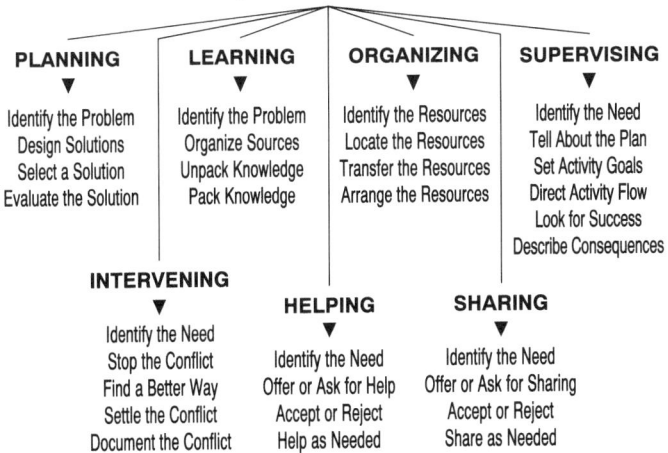

PLANNING ▼

Identify the Problem
Design Solutions
Select a Solution
Evaluate the Solution

LEARNING ▼

Identify the Problem
Organize Sources
Unpack Knowledge
Pack Knowledge

ORGANIZING ▼

Identify the Resources
Locate the Resources
Transfer the Resources
Arrange the Resources

SUPERVISING ▼

Identify the Need
Tell About the Plan
Set Activity Goals
Direct Activity Flow
Look for Success
Describe Consequences

INTERVENING ▼

Identify the Need
Stop the Conflict
Find a Better Way
Settle the Conflict
Document the Conflict

HELPING ▼

Identify the Need
Offer or Ask for Help
Accept or Reject
Help as Needed

SHARING ▼

Identify the Need
Offer or Ask for Sharing
Accept or Reject
Share as Needed

SELF-MANAGEMENT SYSTEM

A Model of How the Strategies Work Together

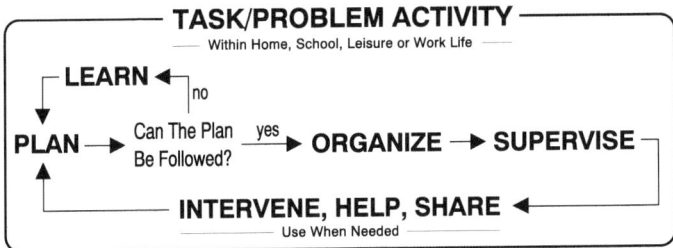

TASK/PROBLEM ACTIVITY
Within Home, School, Leisure or Work Life

LEARN ◄ no

PLAN → Can The Plan Be Followed? yes ► ORGANIZE → SUPERVISE

INTERVENE, HELP, SHARE ◄
Use When Needed

PRINCIPLES OF FAMILY

A Code of Conduct for Family Members

1. **PRINCIPLE OF HEALTH**   Family members have the right to emotional, intellectual and physical health, and the responsibility to promote the same for others.

2. **PRINCIPLE OF REPRESENTATION**   Family members have the right to speak out about the design and implementation of their family activities, and the responsibility to promote the same for others.

3. **PRINICIPLE OF JUSTICE**   Family members have the right to impartial judgment in conflicts, and the responsibility to promote the same for others.

4. **PRINCIPLE OF MEMBERSHIP**   Family members have the right to the participation and cooperation of one another, and the responsibility to provide the same for others.

5. **PRINCIPLE OF QUALITY**   Family members have the right to perform their tasks at a level of excellence, and the responsibility to promote the same for others.

6. **PRINCIPLE OF ADAPTATION**   Family members have the right to change so they can handle existing activities, and the responsibility to help others do so.

7. **PRINCIPLE OF EVOLUTION**   Family members have the right to change so they can function in a wider range of activities and systems, and the responsibility to help others do so.

8. **PRINCIPLE OF CONSERVATION**   Family members have the right to conserve resources so that present and future systems have an increased chance to function according to the Principles of Family, and the responsibility for helping others do so.

TEACHING
Viewed as What Teachers Do to Insure Learning

ESTABLISH CONTINGENCIES

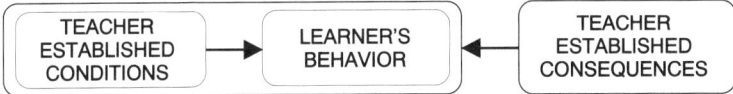

| TEACHER ESTABLISHED CONDITIONS | → | LEARNER'S BEHAVIOR | ← | TEACHER ESTABLISHED CONSEQUENCES |

SO LEARNERS HANDLE ACTIVITIES

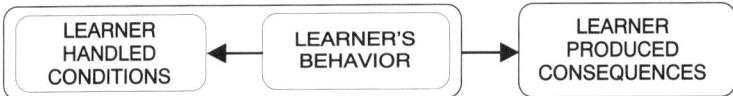

| LEARNER HANDLED CONDITIONS | ← | LEARNER'S BEHAVIOR | → | LEARNER PRODUCED CONSEQUENCES |

TOOLS OF TEACHING
The Components of Teacher-Established Contingencies

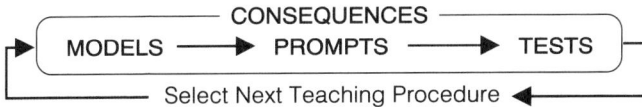

CONSEQUENCES

MODELS → PROMPTS → TESTS

Select Next Teaching Procedure ◄

PROCEDURES OF TEACHING
The Types of Contingencies Teachers Establish to Evolve Behavior

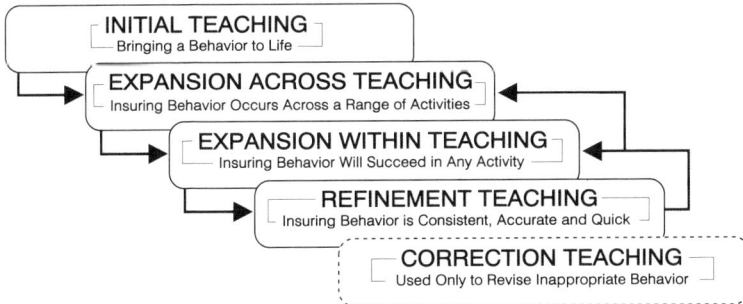

INITIAL TEACHING
Bringing a Behavior to Life

EXPANSION ACROSS TEACHING
Insuring Behavior Occurs Across a Range of Activities

EXPANSION WITHIN TEACHING
Insuring Behavior Will Succeed in Any Activity

REFINEMENT TEACHING
Insuring Behavior is Consistent, Accurate and Quick

CORRECTION TEACHING
Used Only to Revise Inappropriate Behavior

ORGANIZING STRATEGY

1. IDENTIFY THE RESOURCES
   a. What resources are needed?
      (people, materials, tools)
   b. How much of each is needed?

2. LOCATE THE RESOURCES
   a. How can they be located?
      (classification and sources)
   b. Where are they located?

3. TRANSFER THE RESOURCES
   a. Where are they needed?
   b. When are they needed?
   c. How can they be transferred?

4. ARRANGE THE RESOURCES
   a. How can they be arranged?
   b. When should the arrangement
      be completed?
   c. What needs to be returned
      when the task is completed?

HELPING STRATEGIES

——HELPER'S STRATEGY——

1. IDENTIFY THE NEED TO HELP
2. OFFER TO HELP
3. IF OFFER ACCEPTED,
   HELP AS NEEDED
4. IF OFFER REJECTED,
   ACCEPT REJECTION
5. IF THANKED FOR HELPING,
   ACCEPT THANKS

——HELPEE'S STRATEGY——

1. IDENTIFY THE NEED FOR HELP
2. ASK FOR HELP
3. IF REQUEST ACCEPTED,
   PROCEED WITH TASK
4. IF REQUEST REJECTED,
   ACCEPT REJECTION
5. THANK HELPER WHEN DONE

SHARING STRATEGIES

—— SHARER'S STRATEGY ——

1. IDENTIFY THE NEED TO SHARE
2. OFFER TO SHARE
3. IF OFFER ACCEPTED,
   SHARE AS NEEDED
4. IF OFFER REJECTED,
   ACCEPT REJECTION
5. IF THANKED FOR SHARING,
   ACCEPT THANKS

—— SHAREE'S STRATEGY ——

1. IDENTIFY THE NEED FOR SHARING
2. ASK FOR SHARING
3. IF REQUEST ACCEPTED,
   PROCEED WITH TASK
4. IF REQUEST REJECTED,
   ACCEPT REJECTION
5. RETURN ITEM WITH THANKS

SUPERVISING STRATEGY

1. DECIDE ON SUPERVISION
   - a. Is supervision needed?
   - b. What supervision is needed?

2. TELL ABOUT THE PLAN
   - a. What resources are needed?
   - b. What behaviors are needed?
   - b. What consequences are needed?

3. SET ACTIVITY GOALS
   - a. What should our goals be?
   - b. Are the goals possible?
   - c. Does everyone want them?

4. DIRECT ACTIVITY FLOW
   - a. What direction is needed?
   - b. How should direction be given?

5. LOOK FOR SUCCESS
   - a. What has been done?
   - b. What should be done?
   - c. Is there success?

6. POINT OUT CONSEQUENCES
   - a. What ones are or could occur?
   - b. How can they be pointed out?

PLANNING STRATEGY

1. IDENTIFY THE PROBLEM
   a. What is the problem?
   b. What plan needs changing?
   c. Why change the plan?

2. DESIGN SOLUTIONS
   a. What changes are needed?
   b. How can they be designed?
   c. Does anything else change?
   d. Is the new plan clear?

3. SELECT A SOLUTION
   a. What consequences could occur?
   b. Does the plan fit the resources?
   c. Does everyone want to?
   d. Which plan has the best fit?

—— *IMPLEMENT THE NEW PLAN* ——

4. EVALUATE THE SOLUTION
   a. Was the plan followed?
   b. Were there problems?
   c. Is improvement needed?

LEARNING STRATEGY

1. **IDENTIFY THE LEARNING PROBLEM**
   a. What needs to be learned?
   b. Why learn it?

2. **ORGANIZE KNOWLEDGE SOURCES**
   a. What sources could help?
   b. Locate, transfer and arrange them.

3. **UNPACK KNOWLEDGE SOURCES**
   a. Where is the knowledge?
   b. What does the source tell?
   c. Does the knowledge help?
   d. How can it be arranged?

4. **PACK KNOWLEDGE FOUND**
   a. What knowledge is clear?
   b. How can it be arranged?
   c. What more could be learned?
   d. Go to planning?

INTERVENING STRATEGY

1. **IDENTIFY THE NEED TO INTERVENE**
   a. Is there a conflict?
   b. Who can stop the conflict?

2. **STOP THE CONFLICT**
   a. How can the conflict be stopped?
   b. Is more needed?
   c. Who should be the guide?

3. **FIND A BETTER WAY**
   a. What are some better ways?
   b. Select a better way.
   c. Practice the better way.

4. **SETTLE THE CONFLICT**
   a. Is a settlement needed?
   b. What settlements would fit?
   c. Select a settlement.
   d. Monitor the settlement.

5. **DOCUMENT THE CONFLICT**
   a. Was a better way needed? (1-6, 9)
   b. Was a settlement needed? (1-9)

INDUCTIVE THINKING PROCESS

— Thinking Ahead and Thinking Behind —

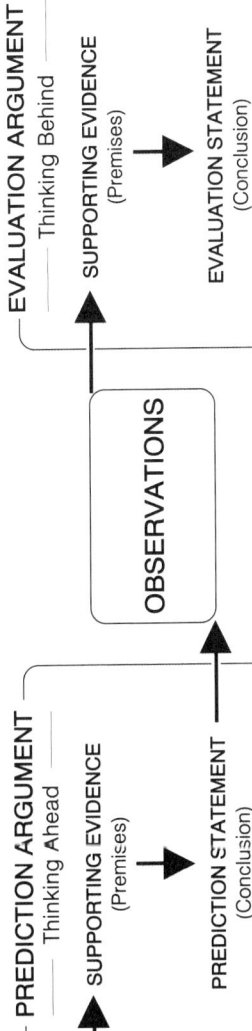

PREDICTION ARGUMENT
— Thinking Ahead —

SUPPORTING EVIDENCE
(Premises)

PREDICTION STATEMENT
(Conclusion)

OBSERVATIONS

EVALUATION ARGUMENT
— Thinking Behind —

SUPPORTING EVIDENCE
(Premises)

EVALUATION STATEMENT
(Conclusion)

KNOWLEDGE TYPES
Four Basic Types With Subtypes

EXISTENTIAL TYPES
▼
What Something Is
(Class Name)
:
What Something Does
(Class Action)

LOCATIONAL TYPES
▼
When Something Is
or Happens
(Location in Time)
:
Where Something Is
or Happens
(Location in Space)

HIERARCHICAL TYPES
▼
What Types Something Has
(Class/Subclass)
:
What Parts Something Has
(Class/Part)
:
What Features Something Has
(Class/Feature)

HISTORICAL TYPES
▼
How Something Changes
(Class Evolution)
:
How Something Happens
(Process, Procedure)
:
Why Something Happens
(Cause and Effect)

—— INTERVENTION DOCUMENT CARD ——

(1) Date: _____   Time: _____   (2) Who Stopped Conflict: _____

(3) Those in Conflict: _____

(4) Description of Conflict: _____

_____

(5) The Better Way: _____

_____   (6) Practiced: Yes   No

(7) Settlement? _____

_____   (8) Completed: Yes   No

(9) Signed: _____

INTERVENING STRATEGY

1. IDENTIFY THE NEED TO INTERVENE

   a. Is there a conflict?

   b. Who can stop the conflict?

2. STOP THE CONFLICT

   a. How can the conflict be stopped?

   b. Is more needed?

   c. Who should be the guide?

3. FIND A BETTER WAY

   a. What are some better ways?

   b. Select a better way.

   c. Practice the better way.

4. SETTLE THE CONFLICT

   a. Is a settlement needed?

   b. What settlements would fit?

   c. Select a settlement.

   d. Monitor the settlement.

5. DOCUMENT THE CONFLICT

   a. Was a better way needed? (1-6, 9)

   b. Was a settlement needed? (1-9)

IS MORE NEEDED?

CONSIDER

1. Does the same type of conflict continue during an activity, across activities, or over days?

2. Does the conflict interrupt the activities of those not involved in the conflict?

3. Does the conflict damage property?

4. Does the conflict put someone in danger?

5. Do those involved have a history of conflicts?

CONSIDER

IS A SETTLEMENT NEEDED?

INTERVENING STRATEGY

1. IDENTIFY THE NEED TO INTERVENE
 a. Is there a conflict?
 b. Who can stop the conflict?

2. STOP THE CONFLICT
 a. How can the conflict be stopped?
 b. Is more needed?
 c. Who should be the guide?

3. FIND A BETTER WAY
 a. What are some better ways?
 b. Select a better way.
 c. Practice the better way.

4. SETTLE THE CONFLICT
 a. Is a settlement needed?
 b. What settlements would fit?
 c. Select a settlement.
 d. Monitor the settlement.

5. DOCUMENT THE CONFLICT
 a. Was a better way needed? (1-6, 9)
 b. Was a settlement needed? (1-9)

HELPING STRATEGIES
—— HELPER'S STRATEGY ——

1. IDENTIFY THE NEED TO HELP

2. OFFER TO HELP

3. IF OFFER ACCEPTED,
   HELP AS NEEDED

4. IF OFFER REJECTED,
   ACCEPT REJECTION

5. IF THANKED FOR HELPING,
   ACCEPT THANKS

—— HELPEE'S STRATEGY ——

1. IDENTIFY THE NEED FOR HELP

2. ASK FOR HELP

3. IF REQUEST ACCEPTED,
   PROCEED WITH TASK

4. IF REQUEST REJECTED,
   ACCEPT REJECTION

5. THANK HELPER WHEN DONE

TEACHING
— Viewed as What Teachers Do to Evolve Learner Behavior —

—— ESTABLISH CONTINGENCIES ——

| TEACHER ESTABLISHED CONDITIONS | ← | LEARNER'S BEHAVIOR | → | TEACHER ESTABLISHED CONSEQUENCES |

SO LEARNERS HANDLE ACTIVITIES

| LEARNER HANDLED CONDITIONS | ← | LEARNER'S BEHAVIOR | → | LEARNER PRODUCED CONSEQUENCES |

—— TOOLS OF TEACHING ——
— The Components of Teacher-Established Contingencies —

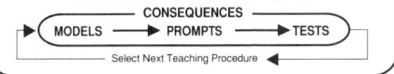

CONSEQUENCES
MODELS → PROMPTS → TESTS
Select Next Teaching Procedure ◄

—— PROCEDURES OF TEACHING ——
— The Types of Contingencies Teachers Establish to Evolve Behavior —

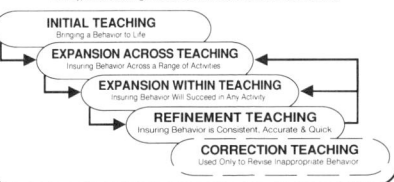

INITIAL TEACHING
Bringing a Behavior to Life

EXPANSION ACROSS TEACHING
Insuring Behavior Across a Range of Activities

EXPANSION WITHIN TEACHING
Insuring Behavior Will Succeed in Any Activity

REFINEMENT TEACHING
Insuring Behavior is Consistent, Accurate & Quick

CORRECTION TEACHING
Used Only to Revise Inappropriate Behavior

SELF-MANAGEMENT
— Viewed as a Set and a System of Strategies —

SELF-MANAGEMENT STRATEGIES
— The Strategies and Their Component Steps —

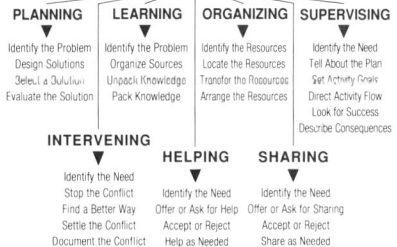

PLANNING	LEARNING	ORGANIZING	SUPERVISING
Identify the Problem	Identify the Problem	Identify the Resources	Identify the Need
Design Solutions	Organize Sources	Locate the Resources	Tell About the Plan
Select a Solution	Unpack Knowledge	Transfer the Resources	Set Activity Goals
Evaluate the Solution	Pack Knowledge	Arrange the Resources	Direct Activity Flow
			Look for Success
			Describe Consequences

INTERVENING	HELPING	SHARING
Identify the Need		
Stop the Conflict	Identify the Need	Identify the Need
Find a Better Way	Offer or Ask for Help	Offer or Ask for Sharing
Settle the Conflict	Accept or Reject	Accept or Reject
Document the Conflict	Help as Needed	Share as Needed

SELF-MANAGEMENT SYSTEM
— A Model of How the Strategies Work Together —

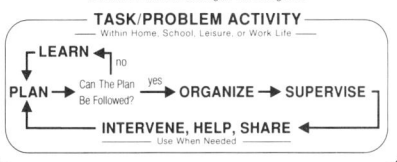

TASK/PROBLEM ACTIVITY
— Within Home, School, Leisure, or Work Life —

LEARN ◄ no
PLAN → Can The Plan Be Followed? → yes → ORGANIZE → SUPERVISE

INTERVENE, HELP, SHARE ◄
— Use When Needed —

SHARING STRATEGIES

——SHARER'S STRATEGY——

1. **IDENTIFY THE NEED TO SHARE**
2. **OFFER TO SHARE**
3. **IF OFFER ACCEPTED,**
   SHARE AS NEEDED
4. **IF OFFER REJECTED,**
   ACCEPT REJECTION
5. **IF THANKED FOR SHARING,**
   ACCEPT THANKS

——SHAREE'S STRATEGY——

1. **IDENTIFY THE NEED FOR SHARING**
2. **ASK FOR SHARING**
3. **IF REQUEST ACCEPTED,**
   PROCEED WITH TASK
4. **IF REQUEST REJECTED,**
   ACCEPT REJECTION
5. **RETURN ITEM WITH THANKS**

©1992 Michael B. Medland

IS MORE NEEDED?

CONSIDER

↓

1. Does the same type of conflict continue during an activity, across activities, or over days?
2. Does the conflict interrupt the activities of those not involved in the conflict?
3. Does the conflict damage property?
4. Does the conflict put someone in danger?
5. Do those involved have a history of conflicts?

↑

CONSIDER

IS A SETTLEMENT NEEDED?

©1992 Michael B. Medland

PRINCIPLES OF FAMILY

—————— A Code of Conduct for Family Members ——————

1. **PRINCIPLE OF HEALTH** Family members have the right to emotional, intellectual, and physical health, and the responsibility to promote the same for others.

2. **PRINCIPLE OF REPRESENTATION** Family members have the right to speak out about the design and implementation of their family activities, and the responsibility to promote the same for others.

3. **PRINCIPLE OF JUSTICE** Family members have the right to impartial judgment in conflicts, and the responsibility to promote the same for others.

4. **PRINCIPLE OF MEMBERSHIP** Family members have the right to the participation and cooperation of one another, and the responsibility to provide the same for others.

5. **PRINCIPLE OF QUALITY** Family members have the right to perform their tasks at a level of excellence, and the responsibility to promote the same for others.

6. **PRINCIPLE OF ADAPTATION** Family members have the right to change so they can handle existing activities, and the responsibility to help others do so.

7. **PRINCIPLE OF EVOLUTION** Family members have the right to change so they can function in a wider range of activities and systems, and the responsibility to help others do so.

8. **PRINCIPLE OF CONSERVATION** Family members have the right to conserve resources so that present and future systems have an increased chance to function according to the Principles of Family, and the responsibility for helping others do so.

©1992 Michael B. Medland

TEACHING GUIDELINES

1. Begin teaching when your children can speak in simple sentences and identify a host of objects and actions.

2. Initially teach one strategy at a time in the order indicated in the book.

3. Start expansion teaching right after initial teaching.

4. Begin teaching strategy elements after initial teaching of all strategies and when your child can read.

5. Refinement teaching occurs with expansion teaching.

6. You can change your teaching plans.

7. Teach so your child loves every minute of it.

8. To teach the older child who can read, begin with family activity planning and present the systems view of the self-management strategies.

© 1992 Michael B. Medland

ORGANIZING STRATEGY

1. **IDENTIFY THE RESOURCES**
   a. What resources are needed? (people, materials, tools)
   b. How much of each is needed?

2. **LOCATE THE RESOURCES**
   a. How can they be located? (classification and sources)
   b. Where are they located?

3. **TRANSFER THE RESOURCES**
   a. Where are they needed?
   b. When are they needed?
   c. How can they be transferred?

4. **ARRANGE THE RESOURCES**
   a. How can they be arranged?
   b. When should the arrangement be completed?
   c. What needs to be returned when the task is completed?

PLANNING STRATEGY

1. **IDENTIFY THE PROBLEM**
   a. What is the problem?
   b. What plan needs changing?
   c. Why change the plan?

2. **DESIGN SOLUTIONS**
   a. What changes are needed?
   b. How can they be designed?
   c. Does anything else change?
   d. Is the new plan clear?

3. **SELECT A SOLUTION**
   a. What consequences could occur?
   b. Does the plan fit the resources?
   c. Does everyone want to?
   d. Which plan has the best fit?

—— *IMPLEMENT THE NEW PLAN* ——

4. **EVALUATE THE SOLUTION**
   a. Was the plan followed?
   b. Were there problems?
   c. Is improvement needed?

LEARNING STRATEGY

1. **IDENTIFY THE LEARNING PROBLEM**
   a. What needs to be learned?
   b. Why learn it?

2. **ORGANIZE KNOWLEDGE SOURCES**
   a. What sources could help?
   b. Locate, transfer, and arrange them.

3. **UNPACK KNOWLEDGE SOURCES**
   a. Where is the knowledge?
   b. What does the source tell?
   c. Does the knowledge help?
   d. How can it be arranged?

4. **PACK KNOWLEDGE FOUND**
   a. What knowledge is clear?
   b. How can it be arranged?
   c. What more could be learned?
   d. Go to planning?

SUPERVISING STRATEGY

1. **DECIDE ON SUPERVISION**
   a. Is supervision needed?
   b. What supervision is needed?

2. **TELL ABOUT THE PLAN**
   a. What resources are needed?
   b. What behaviors are needed?
   b. What consequences are needed?

3. **SET ACTIVITY GOALS**
   a. What should our goals be?
   b. Are the goals possible?
   c. Does everyone want them?

4. **DIRECT ACTIVITY FLOW**
   a. What direction is needed?
   b. How should direction be given?

5. **LOOK FOR SUCCESS**
   a. What has been done?
   b. What should be done?
   c. Is there success?

6. **POINT OUT CONSEQUENCES**
   a. What ones are or could occur?
   b. How can they be pointed out?

INDUCTIVE THINKING PROCESS
— Thinking Ahead and Thinking Behind —

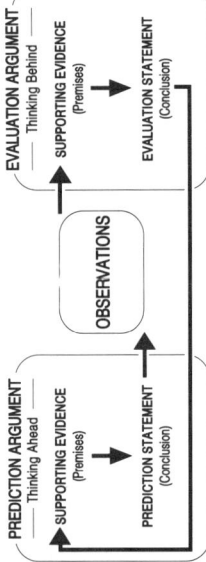

EVALUATION ARGUMENT
— Thinking Behind —

SUPPORTING EVIDENCE
(Premises)

→ EVALUATION STATEMENT
(Conclusion)

OBSERVATIONS

PREDICTION ARGUMENT
— Thinking Ahead —

SUPPORTING EVIDENCE
(Premises)

→ PREDICTION STATEMENT
(Conclusion)

© 1992 Michael B. Medland

NOTES ON RESOURCES

PEOPLE: What skills do they need?
How many are needed?

TOOLS: What kinds?
What quality?
How much of each?

PLACE: How much space?
What lighting?
How much comfort?

TIME: When do you start?
When do you stop?
How much time per day?
How much time for each person?

SYSTEMS THINKING: Change any resource and the others can change.

© 1992 Michael B. Medland

SUPERVISION GUIDELINES

1. Supervise only the steps needed.
2. Lead with questions when possible.
3. If the task can be done in many ways, let those supervised make the decision.
4. Always look for success.

© 1992 Michael B. Medland

KNOWLEDGE TYPES
—— Four Basic Types With Subtypes ——

EXISTENTIAL TYPES
▼
What Something Is
(Class Name)
:
What Something Does
(Class Action)

LOCATIONAL TYPES
▼
When Something Is
or Happens
(Location in Time)
:
Where Something Is
or Happens
(Location in Space)

HIERARCHICAL TYPES
▼
What Types Something Has
(Class/Subclass)
:
What Parts Something Has
(Class/Part)
:
What Features Something Has
(Class/Feature)

HISTORICAL TYPES
▼
How Something Changes
(Class Evolution)
:
How Something Happens
(Process, Procedure)
:
Why Something Happens
(Cause and Effect)

© 1992 Michael B. Medland

INDEX

CREDITS

Developmental Editor

Mark Hubbard
Eureka, California

Assistant Editors

Margo Coleman
Patsy Givins
Eureka, California

Electronic Typesetting

MMT Prepress
Santa Rosa, California

Printing

Bookcrafters
Chelsea, MI

About the Author

Michael Medland has spent over 25 years learning from and teaching children, parents and teachers. Presently, he spends his time teaching, speaking, and doing research on the topics covered in this book. His previous books include *Management of Classrooms* (with Michael Vitale) and *Self-Management Strategies*, a portion of which formed the foundation for *Happier Families*. He can be contacted at (800) 729-6094.